MONEYLIFE

MoneyLife

WORK SMART – HAVE FUN – MAKE MONEY

TONY CAINE

Cover Design by Sinisa Poznanovic
Typeset by Bookhouse, Sydney
Edited by Margie Tubbs
Author Photo by Jolanta Morgan

ISBN: 978-0-6454170-1-2
Digital ISBN: 978-0-6454170-2-9

CONTENTS

FOREWORD

BY WILLIAM D. DANKO, PH.D.

The opening riff of the 1960s song *We Gotta Get Out of This Place*, popularized by The Animals, is my phone's ring tone. The song reminds us about the plight of many, when it describes a dying father who has been slaving his life away. The hope is that there is a better life for the singer and his girlfriend: we gotta get out of this place, if it's the last thing we ever do ... girl, there's a better life for me and you.

This is a timeless desire. We see loved ones slaving, and dying. We see unfulfilled dreams. We ask ourselves whether this is how it has to be. We need a goal to shoot for. But, how can you reach a goal if you don't know what it is in specific terms? "Getting out of this place" makes sense for most people. But, how do you do it? Will you be like a ship without a rudder on the high seas of life, just drifting in the direction the forces push you? Is it as simple as following your dreams?

As a university professor, I have instructed thousands of students to follow their dreams, but not to forget to make a living. In this concise book, Tony Caine provides some sober guidance on how to do just that: enjoy a worthwhile life that allows you to realistically fulfill your dreams.

Life is about Balance. You must accept that we live in a material world, and that it takes money to support a desired lifestyle. But, how much money is necessary to live the life you want to live? In a balanced life, you will be able to enjoy physical and psychological fitness, and nurture positive relationships with friends and family. It comes down to understanding and managing expectations, as we seek a happy life. For certain, happiness is important. It is health, wealth, friendship, and virtue – all good things – that lead to happiness, according to Aristotle. Our level of happiness defines our whole human life!

So, how do we do this?

Tony shares his considerable experience in this book. He shows us how to focus, and overcome obstacles to achieve goals. It comes down to managing your most precious resource: time. He employs some interesting exercises to engage the reader. He also takes us on a mini-MBA tour by highlighting variables we can control and those that we must just accept. He is truly inspired by the serenity prayer: change what we can, accept what we can't, and pray for the wisdom to know the difference.

This book gives good guidance. My hope is that you, the reader, do not ignore it. Again, having taught many students, they often do just that: ignore sage wisdom. Maybe this is just human nature. More than 250 years ago, Benjamin Franklin lamented the same in his essay *The Way To Wealth*, when he concluded: the people heard the advice, agreed with it, and then practiced the contrary.

I say, practice the contrary at your own peril!

Enjoy and embrace Tony's wisdom. You will live a saner life by finding genuine balance.

William D. Danko, Ph.D.
Coauthor of *The Millionaire Next Door,* **and** *Richer Than A Millionaire ~ A Pathway To True Prosperity* **(www.richerthan-amillionaire.com)**

INTRODUCTION

How do we have it all? What does that even mean? Is it having love, happiness, wealth, abs, mansions, Ferraris, freedom and kids?

It's impossible to answer that question. Everyone is different and different things light us up in different ways. Some of us are simply chasing happiness, trying to find love and enjoying the simple things in life with good friends and family, others are chasing wealth and success, some of the crazy ones like me are trying to have it all …

In the past 10 years I've had thousands of conversations with clients to help them figure out what's going to really light them up and change their life for the better. If I could give you brief summary of all these conversations here's what 99.9 per cent of my clients have said to me regarding their desires;

- ▸▸ **More Time:** Freedom to do the things they enjoy
- ▸▸ **More Money:** The cash to live the lifestyle they desire
- ▸▸ **Health**: They want to be happy with how they look and feel

▸▸ **Strong relationships:** They want love, they want great sex, they want to be great people and have great relationships with their friends, family, kids and colleagues.

▸▸ **Success:** They want to get ahead and get really good at their chosen career. They want to be respected and rewarded for the hard work they've put in.

▸▸ **They want to help:** They care about others. They want to try and lift up other people around them and help others who might not be as lucky as them

Is that all? I don't know but it sounds pretty good to me and I'm running with it ...

The hardest part is how do you put it all together at the same time? I've always found it awesome how a juggler can keep all three balls up in the air while having a big, beaming smile on their face. However, I've found that in life we are generally not great at juggling. We go through patches where we are going really well with our work, but our health drops off. Or we are doing well financially and professionally, but our relationships are all out of whack.

It's challenging to stay on top of everything life throws at us while juggling business, family, health, and wealth. Life isn't meant to be a series of **if** and **then**. You can't assume that: *If you can just get that promotion or that business off the ground, then you will get in shape* or *if I can just start earning this amount of money, then my relationships will get better.*

Anyone with experience, knowledge and a decent dose of dedication can start a successful business, make money or get fit. Just like the juggler throwing one ball up and down in the air, it requires them to focus on a single outcome. The key to a successful life is knowing how to pull all the important parts of your life together at the same time and sustainably.

In the pages to come, you'll learn the method that I have developed to enable you to:

⏩ look after yourself and maximise your energy
⏩ build a successful career or business
⏩ grow your wealth and create a legacy
⏩ build a great lifestyle and enjoy amazing experiences

How would your life change, if your work or business ticked these three boxes?:

1. You enjoyed and were passionate about what it is that you do.
2. Your career or business provides you with enough money to live the exact life you want.
3. Your career or business provides you with flexibility and time to spend your days as you please.

So let me get right to it. I've been fortunate enough to build and sell multiple successful businesses all while trying to balance the challenges of running a house, looking after young kids, managing money, staying in shape and trying to have some fun along the way. The key to all of this was:

Knowing my number then finding the BALANCE

By this I mean knowing what type of life I want, knowing exactly how much my lifestyle costs me, then understanding how much I needed to earn from my work to figure out how to make this all happen. This is what I am going to teach you in this book. Once you have learned to discover your number, then your purpose in life will become crystal clear.

After 10 years of research and testing, I have developed a **4-Step Process** that has proven to be the key to building a great life.

▶ **STEP 1**: Generate Energy and Maximise your Health

Maximise the energy you have and maximise what you can accomplish each day.

▶ **STEP 2**: The Number

Understand how much money you need to earn from your career or business, to live the life you desire.

▶ **STEP 3**: Find Balance and Success in your Work

Design a working situation that provides you with the lifestyle and flexibility you desire.

▶ **STEP 4**: Build Wealth and Give Back

Create sustainable wealth and help others along the way.

Why is it that so many of us are dissatisfied with our lives? The problem is we are trying to juggle so much all at once – our families, health, work, business and finances – and we end up getting so overwhelmed and stressed that it's almost impossible for us to actually enjoy the ride. We've been forced to focus too much on some aspects and we end up neglecting other key areas.

The world is changing and people are waking up to the fact that they actually want to have it all. They want a great career, great relationships, wealth, fitness and just to really love life.

In this book, I'm going to show you 'the other way' to live your life. I'll show you how to *enjoy* your life, focus on the most important things and still achieve **everything** you want.

To give you some context, don't worry ... I'm not a 20-year-old single guy, writing this from a resort in Thailand. I'm in the real world, I know what it's like to juggle all of the everyday challenges that life throws at us on a daily basis. My journey, much like yours, is an everyday struggle, but despite setbacks and roadblocks over the years, I've constantly maintained a vision of where I wanted to get to. I've built a life for myself and my family where I'm now fortunate enough to have an amazing balance. And now, I have the opportunity with this book to help others create amazing lives and careers for themselves.

I understand that everyone's journey is different. For some of you reading this, it may feel like there is no hope, or it's too late, or it sounds too good to be true. This book wasn't written to be a silver bullet or an instant life-changer. It's rather a recipe to help you put together a plan of the things you need to do to build and maintain an amazing life. It is possible; you just need the tools to get started.

Twelve years ago, I made a decision that I was going to adopt the new model; the old model wasn't going to work for me. After suffering a heartbreaking accident my whole life had to change. The life I thought I was on track for was quickly taken away from me. This forced me to take a new road, a more challenging path. Ultimately, this event defined me and enabled me to now be in a position where I have been able to help others get started on their journey towards creating their perfect lives.

Thanks for coming on this journey with me. I can't wait to see you completely transform the way you work and live.

THE PROCESS

1

To get started, I want to share my simple 4-Step Process with you. This has helped me and many others create an amazing career and lifestyle.

▶ STEP 1: Generate Energy and Maximise your Health

The first step we are going to address is your health. Without this, everything else falls apart. There's no point building an amazing life if you're not here to enjoy it. This isn't a diet or fitness book – strict diets and hard training regimes aren't sustainable. I'm just going to give you a few tools to help you create as much energy as possible, and maximise what you can achieve.

▶ STEP 2: Knowing Your Number

Would you be happy flying on a plane if you knew the pilot was blind? No? Me neither. But many of us are flying through life blind, not knowing how much money we actually need to live the life we want. The trick lies in knowing your number, understanding exactly how you want to live, what type of wealth you want to create, and then structuring your work to ensure you earn this income every year.

▸ **STEP 3**: Find Balance (and) Success in your Work

The third step in the process is to drill down into your work. Our overall level of happiness is very reliant on how successful we are and how much enjoyment we are having in our working lives. I'm going to give you some strategies that will help you to restructure your work, maximise your success and supercharge your motivation for life.

▸ **STEP 4**: Build Wealth and Give Back

The fourth step we are going to cover is creating wealth and giving back. There's no point in building a great career and earning good money if you don't know how to manage it. None of us want to work forever. I'm going to show you how to build wealth, so if one day you can't or don't want to work anymore, you have enough investment income to sustain your desired lifestyle. Once you have some money, then I want you to give some back. Giving is the ultimate win-win. I'm going to show you how you can start to take action in this area and how it will change your life.

People who say that money can't buy happiness
haven't given enough away yet.

—unknown

YOUR STARTING POINT

Before we get going, I want to do a super quick test to identify where you are starting from on your journey. This is a chance to give yourself an honest assessment of how you think you are performing in each of the key areas of your life.

Be honest when completing the questions below, as this tool is critical in discovering what areas of your life you need to start working on. I don't want you to share this with anyone; it's just for you, it's a chance for you to be honest with yourself. It's also our starting point for making long-lasting positive changes.

Circle the number out of 10 that you believe you are at in the following 5 key areas. A score of 1 indicates you're not doing so well right now; a score of 10 means you're doing amazingly well.

1 ▸ Health

How happy are you with the way you look? The amount of sleep you get? The amount of overall energy that you have? Your general mood? Your motivation levels? Circle your overall self-assessment of your health out of 10.

1   2   3   4   5   6   7   8   9   10

2 ▸ Finances

Are you living in a house that you love? Do you drive the car you want? Do you have money available to regularly travel and do the things that make you happy? Have you got a financial plan in place, to ensure you continually grow your wealth and will be able to provide for your children's education, your own future, and the generations to come after you? Circle your overall self-assessment out of 10.

1   2   3   4   5   6   7   8   9   10

3 ▸ Work and Business

Out of 10, how much are you enjoying work? Are you moving towards your career or business goals? Are you in the right business and earning the money you desire? How stressed are you? Circle your overall self-assessment out of 10.

1   2   3   4   5   6   7   8   9   10

4 ▸ Happiness

How often do you spend time doing the things that really make you happy? Would you say you have a fun life? Do you have things to look forward to in life? Circle your overall self-assessment out of 10.

1   2   3   4   5   6   7   8   9   10

5 ▸ Generosity

Are you fulfilled? When was the last time you went out of your way to help someone else? Giving is about changing your mindset to be conscious that other people need help rather than actually wanting to make an effort to make a positive difference in other people's lives on a regular basis. Circle your overall self-assessment of how generous you are out of 10.

1   2   3   4   5   6   7   8   9   1 0

Now by adding them together, what's your total life score out of 50 at present?

Health _____
Finances _____
Work and Business _____
Happiness _____
Generosity _____

Total _____ **/ 50**

If you are at 10/10 in all the areas, then congratulations! If you're like the 99.9% of the rest of us, it's likely that there are areas where you are doing well and areas where you could use some help. The aim of this book is to help you make incremental changes in all parts of your life, which together will culminate in a whole new outlook and amazing life for yourself. The aim is not to be perfect – no one scores 10/10 in all categories all of the time. That would be impossible and we all go through dark days, weeks, months and years. The aim of this book is to get you to a point where you are at a consistent seven or eight out of 10 in **all** categories, most of the time.

TIP – It's a good idea to revisit this every 90 days. You would be surprised how quickly life can get out of whack and it really helps to realign yourself regularly. You can find templates in the bonus workbook section at the back of this book and if you need help completing this there is also a video tutorial that can be found at tonycaine.com/tools

The New World

The world is changing, fast. The old model, the one that your parents had and maybe you've been made to believe was to study hard at school, get good grades, go to university or do a trade, find a solid job, work your way up, maybe get married, buy a house, raise a family, try save a few dollars so you could hopefully retire in your 60s before you get old, sick and then die … How Boring, what a total snooze! I say Fck that!

That model is being replaced quickly with a new model. Biotech companies are on the cusp of developing technologies that will bring unprecedented increases to the quality and length of human lifespans. This is today, imagine what's going to happen in the next 20 -30 years in Biotech and Longevity science.

All of the things that people are dying from are being researched and solutions are being found to eradicate and prevent fatal diseases and ways to improve early detection. Here is a tiny sample of all the cool shit that's happening in the BioTech industry:

- ▸▸ Stem cell-based therapy for heart failure being licensed.
- ▸▸ Successful trials of implanting an artificial heart.
- ▸▸ Development of DNA-encoded drugs to discover and treat age related diseases.
- ▸▸ Researchers are having early success identifying a small molecule that can be used to rejuvenate the brain for Alzheimer's sufferers.

▸ There's technology being developed to reduce tissue aging, I promise you in 20 years you will see grandmas doing chin ups in gym if they aren't already.

You don't need to know what any of this means, but you can take some comfort in the fact that there are thousands of really smart people and companies all over the world spending countless hours and billions of dollars to make sure we all live longer and healthier lives.

This means you can relax, it's okay, you have time, like a shit load of time. You're not late and you haven't missed out. As long as you look after yourself then it doesn't matter if you're not where you want to be right now, all you need is some information (this book), a plan (this book) , some motivation (this book), then you're good to go!

People are starting to wake up and realise that they can study what they like, do work they enjoy, start a business, change careers frequently, work from anywhere in the world, have a great work/life balance, make money quickly – and all while having an awesome time!

The problem is that a lot of us feel stuck in a certain life arrangement and it's like an anchor constantly holding us down. We've put ourselves in a position where we don't have a lot of options to change things and move towards a different life – a life full of fun, happiness, wealth and fulfillment. Some of you may have bought a house that is too expensive, which means that you need to work hard at a job you don't like just to afford the mortgage. Or you may be living in an area where there is a lot of social pressure to drive a certain car, send your children to certain schools and live in a certain house. So all of this is actually feeding your unhappiness and getting you deeper into debt. Some of you are in the completely wrong relationship that's holding you back from being able to find anything close to happiness but more on this later.

The good news is that no matter how bad your current situation is, as long as you can trust me on the fact that you do have time then you can change things. I'm about to show you how to design an action plan for your life, then take small, slow consistent steps towards designing your amazing life. This isn't going to happen overnight. I don't want you to feel better for just a week or a month or even a year. I'd prefer you to spend a whole year and completely transform your life and work so that you can build a sustainable life forever. My hope is that this book fundamentally changes the way you look at life and work. Not only for you but for the people around you. By fixing yourself and getting to a place of abundance and happiness, you are going to have a huge impact on the people around you. It's contagious; people are going to want what you have and the deal is you have to pass it on.

A common trait amongst people who are winning and enjoying an amazing life is Gratitude and Opendmindess. They think differently to people who are not winning in life. Winners think and say things like:

- ⏵ *Yeah, I'll give that a go!*
- ⏵ *I'm lucky to have what I have, how can I improve the lives of other people?*
- ⏵ *What can I do to make sure my partner and kids can have an amazing life?*
- ⏵ *How can I improve myself every day?*
- ⏵ *What's not working for me; what or who do I need to get rid of in my life that's bringing me down?*
- ⏵ *What do I need to learn to get me from where I am to where I want to be?*

▸▸ *Who can I connect with to help me get to where I want to be?*

▸▸ *How do I take this version of my life to the next level?*

Winners are constantly asking themselves these questions. They are seeking out constant improvement in their lives. In the chapters to come, you are going to learn how to transform your mindset from where it is currently to exactly where you need it to be to live your version of an amazing life.

THE LONG ROAD HERE

3

I suppose I better tell you a bit about me really quickly. Firstly, I am far from perfect. I'm just a guy who has had a massive crack at life and I've stuffed up heaps.

I've made heaps of bad calls but I've been lucky that a few of the good calls I've made have enabled me to build, grow and sell some successful businesses. Most importantly though, through the good, the bad and the ugly I've always done it with a smile on my face and learned a lot.

My philosophy is and has always been: be good to people, work hard and if God can give me a bit of luck, I'll do the rest. Believing is my job, the outcome is his!

I hope my story can motivate you to believe that no matter where you are right now, you can build an amazing life. For me, money is important but it's not the only goal. If I was paid for every hour I get to spend with my kids, then I'd be richer than Warren Buffet. And that's what I'm most proud of.

Growing up in a middle-class family of six kids, I learned to be creative and to think on my feet. Three older brothers, a younger sister and a younger brother created an amazing environment for learning how to share, work together and be resourceful. I watched Mum and Dad work hard just to keep our family afloat. From an early age, I was fascinated by why some people had money, nice houses, cars and went on great holidays, while we didn't. I remember as a young kid watching how hard Mum and Dad worked and it seemed as though we were always *just* making it. As I matured and found work myself, I quickly realised that it wasn't about income, it was about what you did with it. From 14, I had two jobs. I washed the neighbors' cars for money, bought and sold shit, I even worked for a pharmacy delivering medication to the elderly people in nursing homes on my pushbike (yes they let 14 year-olds handle medication back in my day ...). If there was a dollar to be made, I was doing it.

If you've ever met me you know I love to talk, when I used to drop off medication to the elderly they would always rope me in for a chat. I swear by the age of 15 I had tried every single flavour of tea on the planet.

Spending a lot of time talking to elderly people gives you some amazing insights into what life's all about. I remember one time I sat down for another tea with one of the customers, I don't remember his name but I do remember him telling me how, if he had a chance to do it all again, he would do things differently. One thing he said that has stuck with me was that he wished he'd spent more time with his family – that was his major regret. He was proud that he raised a great family and provided for them, but he ended up with way more money than he ever needed and he would have loved to have traded some of those dollars for more time with his family in the golden years. That's a pretty deep conversation for a

14-year-old. I didn't really think about it again until my late 20s and as I started to have a family of my own, but these thoughts came back to me and have maybe shaped who I am and how I think today.

My lifelong goal was to play professional sports. I had watched my older brothers go pro and felt it was always my destiny. At the age of 19, I was selected to make my professional rugby league debut. It was a dream come true, something that I had been thinking about every day since I was five.

I'll never forget that cold Saturday night in the middle of winter in 2006. I had hundreds of family and friends there, all waiting to get off the bench and get on the field and achieve my lifelong dream and make my pro debut. Running onto the pitch wearing the Cronulla Sharks jersey and making my debut was the proudest moment of my life; I finally felt like all my dreams had come true. I had it all planned out, I thought I was set, I was going to go on and have a long and illustrious career and make millions of dollars.

Then, four minutes into my career I took the ball and went for a long kick and **snap**! My leg had swung into an opposing player's body and my entire knee crushed into pieces. There was hardly anything connecting the top half of my leg to the bottom half. I was carried off the field immediately, with my leg in pieces and my lifelong dream crushed. It was all over before It had even started.

I spent the next 12 months in and out of hospital and rehab. While I did manage to return to the playing field for a handful of pro games over the next two years, the knee wasn't the same. It got to a point where I could hardly run – so ultimately, at 21, I retired. The injury ended my career before it had started. My lifelong dream along with the potential of millions of dollars was flushed down the drain.

Problem was, I had put all my eggs in one basket, I didn't have a rich family to lean on and I had no backup plan, so I was essentially screwed.

At such a crossroads, it's fight or flight time. At the time, I was having some dark thoughts about my life. I couldn't understand why all of my dreams had been taken away from me and how life could be so harsh. To be honest, I'd lost all purpose in life. I'd always tried to be a good person, I felt like I didn't deserve this.

Photo Courtesy – Grant Trouville – Instagram @chuckstagram

I remember the day my life changed, and I decided to step up, get my shit together and fight on. I was at the hospital for another operation on my knee to take some screws out or put them in – there were so many operations I lost count. At the time, the hospital was doing renovations and some of the kids in oncology were mixed with general surgery. Seeing all of the sick children and hanging with them while I was recovering made me immediately snap out of my misery and sadness. I remember feeling so guilty and selfish that I was upset about having a bad knee when there were children in hospital fighting for their lives. I was in there for two days, some of these kids had been in and out for two years.

At that moment, everything changed. I vowed that I would never complain about my career-ending injury again and that I would find a way to achieve all the goals I had, no matter what challenges lay ahead. From that moment onwards one of my major goals has been assisting children who are going through tough times. That's really important to me, and, to this day, I still spend time at the children's hospital helping the kids out.

Immediately after leaving the hospital, I had a new lease on life. I had to find a new career. I turned my misery into a chance to reset my life. The good thing about having nothing is that you have nothing to lose, so you can literally try anything. I'd always been fascinated with money, so I decided that finance was going to be my chosen career path. The only problem was that no one wanted a 21-year-old ex-athlete with a banged-up knee and no experience!

I stumbled across a job opportunity for a position in a financial planning academy. No experience was required and they were taking applicants from all walks of life under a type of career-changer program. I applied for a position and miraculously got accepted into the 13-week intensive program. For 13 weeks they throw you into a classroom to learn the trade of financial planning, then leading participants are selected for placement in top financial planning firms across the country.

I remember being in a room full of ex-lawyers, bankers and accountants just trying to keep up. Out of 32 people enrolled in the program, I was by far the least qualified and experienced. But I knew that I could outwork anyone in that room and I had youth and energy on my side. By the end of the 13 weeks, I had climbed the ranks; out of 32 people on the program, I managed to be the second person placed into one of the country's leading financial planning firms – Navigate Financial Group. This changed my life. At Navigate, the Director, Harry Moustakas, taught me the technical craft of how to look after people's money and also, more importantly, how to look after people.

After five years at Navigate, I decided to start my own financial planning business. This was where the fun started. I convinced my wife to use the $20,000 we had earmarked for a home deposit to buy a financial planning business for $200,000. I got a loan for $180,000 and jumped into the deep end. I always wanted an opportunity to start my own business and this was it. I worked 12-15 hours a day for three years and grew the business from its base of $200,000. I sold it for more than $1,000,000 exactly three years later.

This changed everything for us. From then on, my wife and I have been lucky enough to go on and build, scale and sell multiple million-dollar businesses and complete several successful property developments. God's given me the gift of being able to understand how to do these things and I've finally gotten around to writing a book to show others how to build success and wealth in life.

I hope I didn't come across as arrogant by running you through my story but I wanted to give you confidence that I have the runs on the board to help you on your journey to creating an amazing life. Most importantly, I want to show you how quickly your life can change. Deciding to take the plunge and follow my dreams has changed my family's life forever. Hopefully, I can provide you with some inspiration and the belief that this can happen to you too.

So enough about me, let's get back to helping you build an amazing life

We are about to embark on the four-step process of completely transforming your life. Thanks again for coming on this journey with me. I hope the pages to come can give you the tools you need to be the best version of yourself, to find happiness and most importantly compel you to help many others improve their lives.

STEP 1 IN THE PROCESS

GENERATING ENERGY

You're probably wondering how the topic of health has crept its way into a business and wealth book? It's a good question. I don't exercise, eat well and sleep well for abs. I do it for energy. Energy is everything. You look at every single happy and successful person in the world and they will have an abundant amount of energy. Energy is the key to designing a perfect work/life balance and building a successful business.

Think about this simple equation:

1. Good health = energy
2. Energy = the ability to be able to get up earlier and accomplish more in a day
3. More accomplishments = more income and success
4. More income and success = more money and flexibility
5. More money and flexibility = better lifestyle

If you often lack energy and feel lethargic, you will be operating at a slower speed and it will take you longer to accomplish tasks. This means that you will be at work longer so something will have to give, be it catching up with friends, working out, having fun or spending time with your family.

Your body, mind and spirit all together make up the machine that gets you through life. To give yourself the best chance of living well, you need to have this machine operating at a solid seven to eight out of 10 consistently. We can do this by making subtle lasting changes. It's hard to have a great life unless you are healthy; no amount of money can save you from sickness. The key here is finding great balance in your health.

When it comes to physical activity, trust me, I've tried everything. As a former professional athlete, I've been fortunate to have been exposed to the training and dieting methodology that pro athletes use to reach peak performance. As a pro, it's easy to stay healthy and have a six-pack – you are being paid to train; you have people preparing your food and you don't have to worry about actually going to a job.

But for the 99.9 per cent of us who aren't professional athletes, we need a basic plan to maintain long-term health. Over the past 10 years, I've developed a system to enable you to reach and maintain a great level of health. Here's my step-by-step guide:

EXERCISE: Your Physical Activity Plan

Step 1:
Identify two to three different physical activities that you don't mind doing. For example:
Weight training
Walking
Rowing

Outdoor cycling

Surfing

Running

CrossFit

Spin classes

Squash

Pilates

Spin classes

Swimming

Boxing

Soccer

Step 2:

Plug your chosen physical activities into your week. Aim to exercise for **150 minutes** per week. You can break this down however you like, but do try to find 150 minutes somewhere in your weekly schedule, whether it's:

5 × 30 min sessions per week

3 × 50 min sessions per week

6 × 25 min sessions per week.

I like to train in the mornings, as it puts me into a solid mental state, helps me win the morning and provides me with a lot of energy for work. But I'm a morning person and everyone is different. You might be better at night or during the middle of the day. It doesn't matter when you exercise, the key is to find a consistent routine, one that suits your life set up and work arrangements.

Be as practical and as realistic as you can be when planning your training times. For example, if you're planning to train at lunchtime but know that you often get held up at meetings, this isn't an ideal time. You will end up missing your sessions and won't get the benefits. Take some time this week to identify what you don't mind doing for training and how you can schedule 150 minutes into your current week. I'd also encourage you to try and find a team event for one of these sessions. It's healthy to be involved in competition and gives you something to look forward to; it also adds a social element to your week, which leads to other positive benefits in your life.

Step 3

Once you have identified the type of exercise you will be doing every week, I want you to be conscious of your energy output. You won't find what I'm about to say written or published very often, but I **don't** recommend you train too hard. I've been a professional athlete and have pushed myself to the absolute limit thousands of times and it is not sustainable and often leads to injuries.

If you're out of shape, I'd recommend signing up for an intensive four-week program to get you going. These are great for breaking a negative cycle and snapping you into shape. Once complete, the real key is to then design a 'rest of your life program' – not a four, six, eight or 12-week program that makes you feel good but isn't sustainable. As I see it, the problem is that we either go too hard or don't do anything at all – there is often no **balance** in our exercise routines.

I have found that training about 70-80 per cent of my capacity is optimal. At that level, I sweat and I am in a weight loss range, but I'm not completely exhausted to the point that I hate what I'm doing – so exercise is not something that I dread. I never get injured from going too hard; I know how hard I need to go to get a workout without my lungs busting. It's just something that's a part of my life and will be forever.

Sleeping

The first thing I want to say about sleeping is that there is no magic 'one size fits all formula. Scientific research shows that seven to nine hours a night is the optimal amount of sleep required, but I've worked with very energetic people who operate on four to five hours.

Think about it like this: sleeping takes up a third of your life, so the quality of your sleep has a significant impact on you. So it's critical you get it right. Here is a list of my tips to give yourself the best chance for a good night's sleep:

- ▸▸ Go to bed at the same time every night. For me, I try to be in bed by 9 pm every night; it takes me a while to wind down, but if I'm in bed by 9 pm I know I'll be asleep by 10 pm.
- ▸▸ No screen time in bed. Once you are in bed, set your alarm and put your phone on airplane mode. Then put it on the charger, not to be touched until morning.
- ▸▸ Invest in a good bed. My wife and I have invested in the best bed, pillows, and mattress we could find. It's crazy how people will spend $100,000 on a car but won't spend $1,000 on a bed! Think about how much time you spend in your car versus your bed. If you buy a great bed set-up, it will last you a decade; this is one area where it does not pay to be tight.
- ▸▸ Manage the lighting and temperature. Remember that sleeping is a third of your life, so get it right. Make sure you have your room climate controlled so it's not too cold or not too hot; also make sure it's dark enough for you to completely relax.
- ▸▸ Lots of regular sex, why not …
- ▸▸ Finally, I recommend that you take advantage of the apps available to track your sleep. These apps show you

the levels of sleeping depth you fall in and out of in a night. Then you can tweak your environment and bed set-up to get the best quality sleep possible.

Diet

This is not a diet book and – full disclaimer – I am not a qualified dietitian. However, when I played professional sports I was lucky to work with world-class dietitians, including my current dietitian, Jo Turner the owner of NuActive Health, who has shown me how to manage diet effectively.

For me, the key to dieting is **consistency**. I have found a diet that suits my lifestyle and I can use it for the rest of my life. As with exercise, I want you to find a diet that suits you for the next three to four decades, not the next three to four weeks. The diet that works for me is a really simple high protein, low carb diet where I aim for 1,800 calories a day. I don't need to count calories anymore, once you do this for like 30 days, you will be able to easily track your calories. To get started though there are hundreds of online apps such as https://www.myfitnesspal.com/ that make it really easy to plan and track calorie intake.

It might not surprise you that my tips for a healthy diet are all about **balance**. Food makes us happy and why would you give up something that makes you happy? The problem is that being overweight and having no energy makes us unhappy, so we need to find a balance here.

So, here's my formula: **Eat nutritious foods and stick to your calorie goals 80 per cent of the time.** I've been using it for 10 years, and I'll be using it for another 70 years.

Please ensure you consult your GP or a health professional before implementing any specific diet.

Other Key components to Maximise your Energy

Building a Strong Mind

Mental strength isn't something that is specific to soldiers or athletes. We can all improve our mental strength, which in turn improves our mental health and overall level of energy. To finalise this chapter and get you fired up to max out your energy, here are some quick health hacks to strengthen your mind to manage the many challenges that running a business throws at us.

Starting strong

One of my biggest suggestions for anyone is to start every day strong. Build momentum at the start of a day by taking just one small action: make the bed, vacuum, exercise, meditate, walk to the corner to just get moving and have an early win. The simple act of making a conscious decision to get into a routine can make all the difference. Continue to do this every day and gradually step it up; you will begin to notice momentum and see your energy levels shifting.

Managing negativity

One of the other keys to managing your energy is managing your thoughts. We all have bad phone calls, accidents, arguments, flat tyres, etc. These are unavoidable, but your mental recovery time is the key. Work quickly to identify the problem, find a solution, then get back into a peak state. This is critical for managing your energy levels.

Be kind to yourself

I want to finalise this chapter with one last piece of advice which will have the biggest overall impact on your health: **Be kind to yourself**. There are enough people around who are willing to talk bad about you or look at you in a funny way. Don't add yourself to the list. Give yourself a little break and a pat on the back every now and then. Never feel like you are late or behind; there is plenty of time for you to achieve all of your goals and realise your dreams. Just get the vision right, take your time and enjoy the ride. You are doing a lot better than you think.

Four Week Challenge

If you need a hand to swing yourself into tip-top shape, in the back of this book and on tonycaine.com/tools there are templates for a four-week health challenge to help you to build a strong foundation:

- **Exercise**: Aim to complete 150 minutes of exercise per week.
- **Diet**: Maximum one alcoholic drink per weekday. Aim to eat well 80 per cent of the time. Drink 2 liters of water every day. Only one coffee per day.
- **Mental Health**: Spend five minutes every morning in meditation, taking at least 10 deep breaths. Focus on what you are grateful for and visualise an amazing future for yourself.
- **Sleep**: Go to bed at the same time every night; no phone one hour before sleep; sleep for a minimum of 7.5 hours.
- **Relationship Audit:**

TIP – You can access this 4-week challenge templates in the bonus workbook section at the back of this book as well as at tonycaine.com

By the end of four weeks, I guarantee you'll start to feel better. Don't be disheartened if you're not feeling totally better; trust the process and repeat it for the next four months. By the end of six months, you'll look, feel and think like a different person. That's when you'll notice your life-changing.

I know what you may be thinking, forget about this health crap and show me how to make some money, which I will but I promise you need to nail this part of your life to generate the energy you need to put in the work and build the relationships you need to make money and take your life to the next level.

STEP 2 IN THE PROCESS

/5\

THE NUMBER

Okay strap in, I'm about to show you how to get your shit together with your money. For maybe the first time in your life, you are about to understand **why** it is that you do what you do and whether you need to make some changes to either spend less or make more. Don't worry you don't need a masters in economics to learn this shit, I have a masters and I have done the legwork for you. My job is to take all the smart shit out there in all the genius's heads and present it to you in a way that you can understand it and actually make some changes to your money and your life.

Constructing the life of your dreams starts with knowing **Your Number**. Your 'number' is the exact amount of income you need to earn every year to live the exact lifestyle you desire. After completing this chapter, you will identify one of two outcomes:

1. You need to earn more money.
2. You need to adjust your lifestyle expectations.

Before you can become wealthy, you need to know why you are trying to become wealthy. I like to look at this from both an aspirational and measurable perspective, then put a timeframe on setting financial goals.

So to get started, here's a simple two-step process:

Step 1: Understand your financial goals and what you want out of life.

Step 2: Know Your Number

So let's dig a little deeper:

▶ **STEP 1**: Understand your financial goals

There are three kinds of financial goals:

- ▶▶ Aspirational goals (warm and fuzzy stuff)
- ▶▶ Measurable goals (putting numbers to the warm and fuzzy goals)
- ▶▶ Time-stamped goals (attaching a date to them)

Let me show you some examples of **aspirational goals**:

1. Pay your house off.
2. Stay in 5-star hotels and fly business class.
3. Earn great money.
4. Pay for your kids' education.
5. Donate to charity.
6. Retire.

The above goals are examples of how you can get really excited about making changes to your financial situation. Aspirational goals are ones that you can picture, goals that will give you the motivation you need to work hard and be smart with your money. I grew up poor and a holiday for us was a two night trip to a caravan park so to counteract this I am trying to make up for lost time so I like to splurge on trips, When I set goals I get really detailed, fly business class to Lake Como, stay in a suite at the Grand Tremezzo Hotel. See, now I can picture sitting on that plane, I can picture opening up that suite, looking out at that view, doing this literally gets me out of bed or off the couch. So when you do this go deep and have fun with it.

Now let's attach a measure, to turn them into **measurable goals**:

1. Home → Have a $1,000,000 home debt-free.
2. Travel → Spend $50,000 per year on travel.
3. Income → Make $250,000 per annum from your job or business.
4. Kids' education → Save $200,000 to fund your kids' education in full.
5. Giving → Give $20,000 a year away to your preferred charity.
6. Lifestyle → Have a $2,000,000 retirement fund

Now let's attach a date, to turn them into **time-stamped goals**:

1. Home → Have a debt-free $1,000,000 home in 12 years.
2. Travel → In five years, be in a position to spend $50,000 per annum on travel.
3. Income → Within 10 years, build up my business or career so I'm earning $250,000 p/a.
4. Kids' education → In nine years ensure $200,000 is available for kids' education expenses.
5. Giving → In 11 years, I have enough money so I can give $20,000 a year to charity.
6. Lifestyle → In 20 years, semi-retire with a $2,000,000 account to supplement my income.

EXERCISE: Set Your Goals

NAME OF GOAL	WHEN YOU WANT TO ACHIEVE IT BY?	WHAT IS IT GOING TO COST?
		$ -
		$ -
		$ -
		$ -
		$ -
		$ -
		$ -
		$ -
		$ -
		$ -
		$ -
		$ -
		$ -
		$ -
		$ -
		$ -
		$ -

TIP – You can access this goal setting template in the bonus workbook section at the back of this book as well as at tonycaine.com

▶ **STEP 2**: How to work out Your Number

Once you have mapped out your goals and developed a clear and exciting vision, it's time to work out what **Your Number** is.

Let's look at an example …

Let's say below are the expenses for you to live your dream life:

Expense	Annual Cost
Rent/ Mortgage on a place you love	$40,000
Car repayments on your dream car	$22,000
Groceries & Entertainment	$30,000
Household and clothing costs	$10,000
Holidays	$25,000
Investments for future wealth creation	$20,000
Kids Education	$25,000
Insurance	$4,000
Medical	$4,000
Other	$20,000
Total	**$200,000**

This household or individual would need to take home **$200,000** (after tax) to live the life of their dreams. That means **The Number** that they need to earn every year before tax is **$330,000** (you will need to do the tax conversion for whatever state or country you reside). This number now becomes their north star and they need to plan around earning this.

Now you can work on your life and career design to find balance and peace of mind knowing that if you can earn this income in your career then everything will be fine.

Your number could be anything, you might be chasing the FIRE (Financially Independent, Retire Early) strategy which means $50,000 a year is enough or you may want to live an extravagant life that costs $3,000,000 a year. The most important thing is that it's unique to you and that:

- ▸▸ You find the balance between what's going to make you are willing to work for and what makes you happy
- ▸▸ The number is achievable

Here's a real-life example from me. The first business I started, I was working myself into the ground, I was making lots and lots of money, however, I was caught in a trap where I was earning twice as much as what I needed but I was killing myself and was miserable. Once I realised this, I then decided to sell a part of the business off, my income was reduced temporarily but my happiness and lifestyle increased tenfold.

This is the importance of the number, it's like a stress reliever. If you take the time to run the numbers properly, work out what's going to make sure you can live the life you want today then you will be able to plan for a great future.

I can't underestimate the clarity you will gain in your work from simply knowing **Your Number**. It becomes your North Star in everything you do. Moving forward, for every major business or career decision you can ask yourself: *Does the outcome of this decision align with what I need to earn and synchronise with what's going to make me happy?*

Most of us do things the wrong way around. We get stuck in a structure and learn to live with what we earn and don't do anything about it. In this book, I'm going to try to convince you to decide on a life that you want, then structure your career to ensure you earn the required amount of money every year.

In the earlier example, that couple is able to travel, educate their kids, live, eat, drink, wear, and drive whatever they want. And that is the key. You need to know your number, then make the changes in your life to enable you to live your life the way you choose.

There are a thousand ways to make more money and I'll show you how. But first, you need to complete the following exercise and know your number, to understand why you are working hard and trying to earn more.

EXERCISE: What's Your Number?

This exercise will assist you to identify your number. On the following page, I have a budget planner that I would love you to complete. Here is the step by step guide of how to complete:

▸ **STEP 1**. Complete your current budget as your monthly expenses are now.

▸ **STEP 2**. Based on your goals that you've just set, circle and add the expenses you need to upgrade.

▸ **STEP 3**. Complete a revised budget that's going to give you the life you want.

▸ **STEP 4**. Multiply the expenses by 12 to give you the annual number.

▸ **STEP 5**. Now you know Your Number and now we need to help you earn this!

	STEP 1.	STEP 2.		STEP 3.
EXPENSE NAME	MONTHLY AMOUNT	UPGRADING Y/N		NEW MONTHLY AMOUNT
EXAMPLE MORTGAGE/RENT	$ 2,000	(YES) / NO		$ 4,000
MORTGAGE/RENT	$ -	YES / NO		$ -
ELECTRICITY/GAS	$ -	YES / NO		$ -
WATER/GARBAGE	$ -	YES / NO		$ -
VEHICLE PAYMENT	$ -	YES / NO		$ -
VEHICLE INSURANCE	$ -	YES / NO		$ -
GAS/TRANSPORT	$ -	YES / NO		$ -
GROCERIES	$ -	YES / NO		$ -
ENTERTAINMENT	$ -	YES / NO		$ -
TELEPHONE	$ -	YES / NO		$ -
CABLE/INTERNET	$ -	YES / NO		$ -
CREDIT CARD	$ -	YES / NO		$ -
LOAN PAYMENT	$ -	YES / NO		$ -
PET	$ -	YES / NO		$ -
PERSONAL	$ -	YES / NO		$ -
MEDICAL	$ -	YES / NO		$ -
TRAVEL	$ -	YES / NO		$ -
TOTAL	$ - P/M		TOTAL	$ - P/M

STEP 4. X 12

EQUALS

$ _____ P/YR

STEP 5.

HERE IS YOUR NUMBER

You can access this template in the bonus workbook section at the back of this book and if you need help completing this, there is also a video tutorial that can be found at tonycaine.com/tools

You have to get on the same page as your partner

Let's look at one more example of how things can break down and go wrong:

Let's say the husband wants a Mercedes, a $2m home and to put his kids through private school. This means they need to earn $400,000 per annum which requires him to work 60 hours a week. He is okay with this. But his wife isn't fussed about where she lives, believes public education will suffice and that it's more important to have her husband around more. This is an example of a conflict I come across almost daily. There needs to be harmony in what you both want and what you are both willing to do to achieve a certain lifestyle. In other words, make sure that everyone in the household is on the same page.

It's all about **balance**. When planning your life, of course you need to know your number; but it's equally important to make sure you have an understanding of what it's going to take and that all parties are okay with this. If they are not, then you need to continue to dial down your expenses until they match a level of income based on your achievable work output.

Timing is important too, as I remember from when I started my first business. Even though it was my business and I was the one there all day, my wife and I needed to be a team. We both agreed that, for a short period of time, that we were both okay with me working 12-15 hours a day, to do what it took to get the business off the ground and set us up financially.

To be successful, there comes a time when everyone needs to push themselves. So it's critically important to ensure that you communicate what's going on with all parties involved in the relationship. In step three, I'm going to show you how you can start designing a career that aligns with your goals, values, and income requirements.

To summarise, here is the framework for knowing your numbers:

1. Identify the type of life you live and what it's going to cost you.
2. Identify how much work that is going to take, what sacrifices will need to be made to earn that money and whether you are willing to do that.
3. Identify whether your current career or business will provide you with the opportunity to achieve the level of income you desire.

Continue to tweak your living expenses and expectations against the output required to earn this money, until you find the sweet spot between what you desire versus what you are willing to do. This is where happiness lies; once you know **Your Number**, it becomes a lot easier to get out of bed early, put up with that crappy client or work late when you don't feel like it because you have a clearly defined reason as to why you are doing what you are doing.

Next, I want to show you how to create the perfect work/life balance with your career. Once we nail down how to design your perfect career then we are going to be able to generate the income you need to build the wealth you need to live the life of your dreams.

STEP 3 IN THE PROCESS

6

FIND BALANCE AND SUCCESS IN YOUR WORK

Finding the right **balance** in your work will have a huge impact on the overall happiness of your life. The happiest people I know are the people who can structure their workweek to suit their lifestyle to maximise their success and income.

When I wrote this book I was contemplating putting this section about your career at the front of the book as it makes such a big difference on people's general energy and their happiness.

The magic lies in finding the right balance between working enough to be successful and earn the income you need but at the same time not completely sacrificing your health, relationships and happiness. Finding the right *balance* in your work has a huge impact on the overall happiness of your life.

Work is hard and we are all burdened by commitments and responsibilities which hold us back from chasing our dreams. I am a realist – don't worry I'm coming at this from a realistic point of view. I'm not blogging from a café in Thailand without a worry in the world. For me, at this very moment it's 5am, freezing cold outside and I'm in the home office trying to press these laptop keys quietly so I don't wake up the kids. I'm trying to get some writing done before I head to the gym and then off to work to run my companies. I have two kids that want to spend a lot of time with Dad, I have the normal family issues that we all face. So don't worry, in this chapter I'm assuming you're already stressed out, have no time a and have huge responsibilities hanging over your head.

I'm not going to encourage you to quit your job tomorrow and pretend to you that you can make millions trading crypto from Bali. Instead, I'm going to show you how to get into your work groove and find a way to enjoy your work a and create a balanced lifestyle that provides the right mix of:

- ▶▶ Motivation
- ▶▶ Happiness
- ▶▶ Income
- ▶▶ Balance
- ▶▶ Growth
- ▶▶ Fulfillment

I've been really fortunate to have my work/life balance set up exactly the way I want it, but to get there I had to work extremely hard. I don't think there was a single day in my twenties where I didn't work. The reason for this was that I knew, even before I had kids, that when I did eventually have them I'd want to be able to spend a lot of time with them. So, I had to put in the work early to ensure when they came, I was in a good financial and lifestyle position to watch them grow up … Whilst I'm not a billionaire financially, if I put a value on the amount of quality time I get to spend with my family, I'd be the richest person on the planet.

One of the main reasons I'm able to do this is because I haven't fallen for the forbidden income trap ...

The Income Trap

The income trap is the killer of happiness. I've seen it ruin many relationships, destroy people's health and it's the single biggest thing that throws our lives out of whack and into chaos. What is it? It's the trap of working too hard and sacrificing other areas of your life in the pursuit of income that you don't need.

Have you ever heard someone say or have you said to yourself; if I can just get that next promotion then everything will be fine? Or if I can just build this business to this point then I'll have time for my wife and kids? This is The Income Trap. The trap is that the day may never come and if it does, what has it cost you?

No matter how busy you are, or how busy you think you are, the work will always be there tomorrow, but your friends might not be.

— Anonymous

For example, let's take a senior-level solicitor trying to make the partner level at the law firm he's been working at for the past eight years. Let's say this man has two boys aged seven and five and has been married for 11 years. Currently, he's sold himself the story that it's okay for him to work 70-hour weeks because if he can just make partner-level his salary will increase from $250,000 to $450,000 and all of his problems will be solved, right? Wrong!

Let's say our lawyer friend spends the next five years of his life and does make it to partner level. Let's have a look at what this has cost him:

➤ The missed opportunities to spend that quality time with his kids at those amazing ages.

➤ The missed opportunities to spend time with his partner and make sure that she was enjoying life and that she also could do the things that made her happy.

Now despite the qualitative cost of our friend missing out on all those amazing times, what happens if it's all too little too late that his relationship has broken down to a point beyond repair? Now this man has to go through a separation and the family assets he worked so hard for are being divided anyway.

Would this person not have been better to find the *balance* in his work a lot earlier on and try to find a sustainable way to build his career without sacrificing so much?

This is a classic example of someone caught up in the income trap.

Another common example I see is when a couple tries to 'keep up with the Joneses.' Here, I see people so focused on maintaining an artificial standard of life doing anything it takes just to look the part, without considering what it's costing them in their quality of life. We all get caught up from time to time, I've been there and bought things I don't need, trying to prove a point and impress others, if you could avoid making this mistake you will be far better off.

The Number

In the previous chapter, we went through an exercise to determine the amount of money you need to do all the things that you and your family want to do and to invest in your future. Once you know this figure you can reverse engineer it into calculating what you need to be doing to bring this money home.

The Question is:

Does my current job or business have the ability to give me the income I require? If not, you need to look at pivoting or making changes so you can earn this money or adjust your expectations. I need to reiterate here how important it is to know **Your Number**. If you haven't already go back and do the work to find out Your Number. If you need help, head to tonycaine.com/tools and watch the video tutorial and download the working out **Your Number** template. When you know **Your Number** then it helps you make both short and long term decisions about your career.

Now that we know the importance of knowing Your Number and avoiding the income trap, I want to focus on the two different options we have when it comes to building a career – those being:

1. Self Employed

2. Employee

After working with thousands of people over a decade and personally working as an employee for some of the biggest companies in the world such as Salesfroce as well as building, starting and selling multiple businesses, my assessment of which option is better is, it depends …

It's really dependent on the person, there are so many pros and cons and I still believe that there is no better or worse option, it just comes down to the individual's circumstances, timing and preference. For some people, it's in their DNA to start, build and run companies. Others are natural leaders, thriving in a corporate framework where they don't have to worry about the actual logistics of running the company and can instead focus solely on the role they have inside of the company.

The good news is you can have amazing success with either starting your own company or working within an organisation – the key is being in the right structure that suits your natural skillsets.

I think everyone needs to look at themselves as a corporation, regardless of if you are running your own company or are an individual in an organisation. You should be considering yourself as your own personal brand with a value that rises as you grow.

Technically, If you start and run a company, you are an *entrepreneur.*

If you work in a company, instead of looking at yourself as just an employee, you should be looking at yourself as an *intrapreneur.* This essentially means you are a "self-employed" person within a company and encourage employees to think of themselves as their own brand and the company you work for is a client you contract your services to. This tiny shift in your mindset will completely change the way you work. As an employee, you may look at a self-employed person with envy as they have full control over their day or have a big exit from a business. But as an employee, what you need to focus on is the value of your own personal brand and what you can do each and every day to make sure that the value of *"your brand"* is increasing, to ensure you can earn more from the company that has the benefit of using your services. If, for whatever reason, that company is not willing to pay the price (annual salary) you think you're worth, then what changes do you need to make to ensure you are working at the right company getting paid what you are worth?

Skills Alignment

Essentially the structure you work under, be it either self-employed or an employee, should not hold you back from achieving all of your goals and living the lifestyle you want to live. I have worked with just as many successful employees as I have successful business owners. I've also seen many people who started off extremely unhappy as a business owner or employee but decided to make the changes necessary to design the lifestyle they desired. The key is making sure your goals and skillsets are aligned with your work to give you the best chance to maximum success. I believe this is where most people let themselves down. If your career isn't in line with your natural skill set your growth will always be limited. You need to sit back and ask yourself the following questions:

- Do my natural skills compliment my line of work?
- If I did everything right over a long period of time would the organisation I'm working for reward me financially with what I deserve?
- Is the current work I'm doing having a positive or negative effect on my personal brand and image?
- Is the work I'm doing in line with my key values?
- If I did everything right in my company and worked my butt off for the next 5-10 years would all of my financial and career goals be achieved?
- What is missing in my skillset to take me to the next level? What is the key difference between the people who I want to emulate versus what I'm doing?
- Who do I need to speak to and seek guidance from to get me to where I want to be in my career?

When reviewing your career and weighing up your options, I know how hard it can be to put your finger on what you should be doing with your life. I think there is a very small percentage of the population who know from day one exactly what they want to do with their lives. For the majority of us, we are doing our best in whatever line of work we have fallen into for whatever reason.

I wish I could talk to everyone before they fall into their careers and explain the importance of doing something you *like*. See how I used the word *like* not love? I don't believe many people are doing the work they love. I believe you should save the stuff you love for fun and instead try and find something that you like (not love) to make a career out of.

For example, I love snowboarding. It's my favourite thing to do in the world. But if I had to do this for a job and be out in the cold every day teaching other people how to snowboard, I would fall out of love for snowboarding pretty quickly. I think this is where a lot of people make the mistake of trying to turn their hobbies into careers. As a result their favourite things to do becomes a chore. A great way around this is to look at trying to work in something that branches off what you love.

Using a snowboarding example:

In another life, if I wasn't doing what I'm doing today, I would have loved to have been a snowboard photographer or publish a snowboarding magazine that would keep me close to my passion without taking away the enjoyment. You need to have a high level of interest in your industry otherwise it's going to get dull pretty quickly.

Another fantastic way for you to realise if you are in the right industry is to do a values reconciliation. This is reviewing a list of values and cross-checking to see if your values are in synergy with the type of work you are doing.

Discover Your Key Values

By knowing what your key values are, you can then cross-check if your work is in line with your values. Once you've done this, then you can rule out jobs or career options that aren't aligned and move your focus towards jobs and careers that are more closely aligned with your key values. For example, I have highlighted what someone's key values are and then broken them down to show you how this can influence career decisions:

Example – Key Values

1. **Achievement** – This individual is never *just* going to want a 9-5 job; they want to have a line of work with growth, which provides them with a clear path to get exactly where they want to be.
2. **Challenge** – Again, this person is unlikely to do the same role for 50 years. They need to be challenged in their business or career and find a role that is constantly going to test them and stretch their capabilities.
3. **Contribution** – This person isn't ever going to be a part of a business that is purely profit-focused. This person needs to be part of an organisation that is making a positive difference in the world.
4. **Family** – This person values family and therefore isn't going to be in a job or position that means they have to travel interstate and overseas all the time. They value being around their family, so they may be unhappy in a role that pulls them away from a highly prioritised value
5. **Fun** – This person wants to enjoy their work, it's not only about the numbers. While it's quite obvious they are ambitious, they also want to enjoy the ride and have fun with the work they are doing, and the people they are working with.
6. **Honesty** – this person will get uptight and anxious if they are being dishonest, meaning they are never

going to do well in a company that doesn't have a positive corporate responsibility. For example, this person won't do well or be happy working in a high-pressure sales environment where the consumers who are buying a product may be disadvantaged.

7. **Stability** – Although this person is ambitious, they also value stability. This means that whilst they are going to work hard, take risks and challenge themselves to get ahead, they are also going to want a certain level of stability in their life to ensure they will be okay in the long run.

Do you see how this method of values reconciliation could either confirm you are either working in the right or wrong job or industry and potentially help you narrow down what line of work you should be doing?

This is crucially important. Unless you are working in harmony with most of your key values, you will always live with this internal battle between your values and your career. The happiest people I know have found the perfect *balance* between what they do for a living and how this job or career represents their values on a daily basis.

Now that we have looked at your values and given you some motivation to look at your career from a different perspective, I want to spend some time covering off the four key elements you need to find satisfaction in your work or business to be happy and successful. I want you to be energised by your work and restructure your working life so you can get into an amazing groove, find happiness and sustainability and be financially rewarded for it.

Work is work and that will always be the case. This book is about finding the *balance* and showing you how you can make your career or business an 8/10 and sustain this. I believe for you to have sustainable happiness and success in your work, your work needs to provide you with four key elements:

1. **It compliments your natural skill sets and personality.**
2. **It provides you with variety and challenges you.**
3. **Your line of work has the potential for you to earn the income that you desire.**
4. **It suits your lifestyle**

Now let's dive deep into these one by one.

Career Principal 1 – Your line of work compliments your skill sets

I've come across countless examples where I see someone and think *'you would be great at that,'* or I see someone and feel for them, as their natural skill sets do not compliment their line of work at all. For example, let's say you are a people person and get energy from being around others, but your work is office-based and you're stuck behind a desk, which doesn't allow for your natural skillsets to be seen. We all have unique strengths and weaknesses. It's remarkable to me in my research and experience how many people are working in careers and jobs that have no synergy with their natural skillsets.

EXERCISE:

Start by narrowing down your top five to seven skillsets. It makes it easy to work out if you are in the right career or might need to look at a change. The most typical example I see is where people have gotten comfortable in their role, get used to the income, and are just there to get paid. There's nothing wrong with this if it makes you happy, but you don't want to grow old and regret not trying to find a more suitable career you could have enjoyed and excelled in. As an example, let's take a specific set of skills and look at what careers they may best be suited to:

Example 1 – Natural Skill Sets:
Go-Getter
Sales
Multitasker
Strategic Planner
Motivator
Decision Maker

If I was coaching this person I would suggest that they would have a very good chance of starting and running their own business or becoming a CEO. We know that being self-employed requires making hard decisions, the ability to sell a product or service, a lot of motivation, multi-tasking and strategic planning. So, if these skillsets come naturally to someone, it is likely they would succeed in business. Alternatively, based on these skillsets, someone would thrive in a senior role within an organisation.

Example 2 – Natural Skill Sets:
Interviewing
Team Building
Organiser
Good Time Management
Conflict Management
Conflict Resolution

If I was coaching this person I would suggest they possess the skills of a manager. Any great team needs the right people, strong leadership, organisation, conflict management and resolution, along with structured timelines to achieve objectives. Therefore, the above traits would suggest a natural leader and a manager. If they were looking to go into business for themselves, they may want to find someone with the skills of Example 1 to help them to drive the business while they manage the business.

Once you work out what your skillsets are you need to gravitate towards them. It may take some time to change what you do for work but I promise that for your long-term happiness and sanity you need to start making professional arrangements that come naturally to you. This should be one of your highest priorities in life, as the difference this will have on your mental health over the long term is immeasurable.

Career Principal 2 – It provides you with variety and challenges you.

Challenge = Growth, when we are being challenged, we are growing, when our work is not challenging us, we are static. There needs to be a *balance* between challenge and stress, as too much stress is harmful, but not enough challenge in your work can be equally as dangerous. A large cause of unhappiness in the world is a result of people who are disappointed in themselves because they are in the exact same spot or worse than they were a year ago. The reason for this is that they didn't put their hand up for a challenge and instead have taken the simple option to continue with what they were doing.

How many times have you said to yourself, *'this time next year I'll be in a better position'* or set some lofty and exciting new year's resolution that fell by the wayside within weeks? The reason for the lack of growth is the lack of challenge, you can't do the same thing year in year out and expect significantly improved results.

The three-Year Challenge

I believe it takes three years of hard work, dedication and complete commitment to a cause to completely change the course of the rest of your life. There's no rush to start this challenge, but once you are really clear on the career you want to be successful at then you need to decide that it's your time to shine and you're going to go for it. If you are willing to make some sacrifices for three years and throw your life into something, it can completely change the course of your life. Usually, there is a catalyst for you to decide to change your life. For me, it was the birth of my first daughter. I made a conscious decision that I was going to build an amazing life for my family and make sure that I had the time and money to have amazing experiences with them. For others, it could be a relationship breakdown, beating an addiction, marriage or tragedy. It doesn't matter what causes you to make a decision but everyone in the history of the world who has ever been successful has gone through a minimum three-year push.

I love nothing more than seeing one of my clients embark and complete their three-year push. You have no idea what can be accomplished in three years if you throw your whole life into something. When you decide to go for it, make sure whatever you are working towards is personalised to *you* and fits your long-term plans. It's about making a conscious decision to go to the next level. It may be that MBA you need to study to get to the next level in your company or a promotion application you have been putting off, the language you want to learn, the career change you know you need to make or the online course you need to enrol in. I've seen and coached hundreds of people through this and every single time they have decided to dedicate themselves to something for three years, their whole life has changed.

It will seem weird, people around you may try to talk you out of it and look at you differently but you need to embrace being uncomfortable for a while. This is where the growth occurs. The reality is 90 per cent of people will never decide to transform their lives. I hope you are the 10 per cent …

Napoleon Hill once said:

"Tell me how you use your spare time, and how you spend your money and I will tell you where and what you will be in ten years from now"

When you decide to dedicate your life to something there will be short-term sacrifices. The key is to communicate with your loved ones openly and honestly, to let them know that you are going to give your all at something for some time and that you would love their support. Initially, they may try to talk you out of it, only because they love you and don't want to see you get hurt if you fail but once you show them your dedication and start to make progress they will turn into your cheer squad. If you have negative people in your life that are constantly holding you back, now might be the time for you to break away. When you make the conscious decision to go for it, you need to make sure you have the right people in your corner.

It doesn't matter how bad your starting point is, you could be homeless, illiterate, injured, or going through a horrific life circumstance right now and as hard and painful it is, you just need to have the faith that in three years your life can be completely transformed. One year is too short. You can make huge progress in the next 30 days and 12 months but three years is the time it takes to conduct a life transformation across all areas of your life.

You can find a template to access a three-year challenge template at the back of this workbook and at tonycaine.com/tools

10,000 Hours (10 Years)

You may have heard this phrase before and if not I'd highly recommend picking up the book "Outliers" by Malcolm Gladwell. Throughout the publication, Gladwell repeatedly mentions the "10,000-Hour Rule", claiming that the key to achieving world-class expertise in any skill, is, to a large extent, a matter of practicing the correct way for a total of around 10,000 hours.

Essentially, this is where the great get separated from the good or very good. If you've completed the three-year challenge and completely committed to a job, business, project, course, language or whatever it is, you will develop a whole new set of life skills and most importantly, a sense of self-gratification you have never experienced before. More often than not, the results you receive and the income you will now start to earn will become addictive and you will *want* to go to the next level.

You've now had a taste of how the other half lived and proved to yourself that your ability is way more powerful than you may have thought it was just three years ago. If you have ever watched the Tour de France, to win the race at some point the winner has to separate from the pack. The riders will be moving in a pack, then all of a sudden there will be a rider who breaks away. You can physically see the pain on their face from the effort pulling away and staying ahead. This is the same in life and it is what happens when you create separation from the old you and the people you used to compare yourself to. You are making a conscious decision to take charge and this is where the magic happens.

Once you have broken away from the pack, pushed yourself for three years, what the superstars in any field do is take it to an even higher level. They dedicate themselves for another seven years to their chosen line of work to achieve expert level. They narrow in and focus on an exciting challenge in their line of work that is going to take them to the next level, spending these seven years laser-focused on what's going to change the course of their working life and provide them with variety and an abundance of income.

Career Principal 3 – Your career has the ability for you to earn the income that you desire.

Now that we have looked at your skillsets and demonstrated the benefits of doing challenging work, we want to look at making sure that your line of work or business can provide you with the income that you desire. The reality is that some lines of work have a ceiling of income; hard work alone isn't the answer.

> *If you are one of those people who believe that hard work and honesty alone will bring riches, perish the thought. It is not true. Riches, when they come in huge quantities, never come as a result of hard work. They come, if they come at all, in response to definite demands, based upon the application of definite principles, and not by chance or luck.*
>
> **—Napoleon Hill**

In other words, there are only so many hours in the day, so you need to work smarter not harder. As we have just explored, there will always be a tough phase of a minimum of three years where you need to push ahead and get established, but life is not as simple as the hardest worker always wins. No one wants to have to work 80 hours a week for the rest of their lives. The whole aim of the game is to find the *balance* between doing meaningful work you love and are good at. The irony is – the harder you work to get established in the early days the easier it gets and opportunities come to you and you can earn the income that you need to achieve your goals with less effort. You need to access your current working situation and honestly ask yourself this question:

At some point in the future, will my current line of work or business provide me with the opportunity to earn the income that I desire whilst living the lifestyle that I want?

This is such a powerful and confronting question and you need to be able to answer it in full. For example, let's say you're a banking executive and the opportunity is there to earn the income you desire but it would mean working 70 hours a week forever, which isn't your desired lifestyle. Therefore, your answer to this question is a flat *no*. If you are a part-time personal trainer, you may have a great lifestyle, enjoy the hours you work, enjoy the holidays you have but know it's never going to provide you with the income you need, so your answer is also *no*.

The first step in this process is identifying and understanding what you're working with. Most people are flying blind and haven't stopped to think about this. It's a shame because it's so critical. You can waste decades in the wrong line of work, never knowing what you are doing day in day out for a decade and never getting to where you want to be. It saddens me that people live like this and I hope it hits home with you and puts some fire in your belly to start putting together an action plan to get that cash!.

A lot of the most successful people in the world have multiple income sources, so as they say, you don't need to quit your day job. Using the examples above with the banking executive and the part-time worker, they may love their work and want to continue this, but the executive isn't happy sacrificing so much of their free time, and the part-timer isn't willing to work more because they love their lifestyle. That's fine, but there's really only two options:

1. Reducing your expenses
2. Alternative sources of income

Starting with reducing your expenses, remember that time is just as valuable as money. If you place a high value on your time and don't want to sacrifice it with work, you need to have a really good handle on your expenses to ensure that what you are earning is covering the lifestyle you are after and be okay with living a really simple and modest lifestyle.

Secondly, a lot of the most successful people I work with make money while they sleep. The money they earn isn't solely linked to their output and the goal for everyone should always be to make more money while you sleep than you can spend while you're awake.

This is one of the biggest mindset shifts that you can make. Once you understand that you can make money without having to work for it, it unlocks a whole new world for you.

As an example, I have a client named Adam. He is a crane driver and when we first met he was earning good money, about $110,000 per year. Not bad at all, but he was working six days a week and it was taking a toll on his family and his health. He was overtired, out of shape and never had any energy. When we first met, I asked him why he was working so hard, he said he was saving up to buy a home. I asked him the question:

At some point in the future, will your current line of work provide you with the opportunity to earn the income that you desire whilst living the lifestyle that you want?
His answer was a flat no.

So we put together a plan to make changes, we decided that a new home right now wasn't going to change his life one bit. He could rent the house he wanted instead of having to buy it. We looked into the idea of buying his own crane, as opposed to working on a salary for a crane company. Adam had been in the industry for 10 years and knew everything there was to know about cranes and had a lot of industry contacts so it was a pretty safe bet that he would get work if he went self employed.

TIP: See in this example Adam had industry experience and contacts, when starting a business, this is not mandatory but is a huge help and will significantly increase the odds of you succeeding.

So, six months later, Adam had found a crane, organised finance and bought the crane to start his own business instead of driving someone else's crane at an hourly rate. We spent a lot of time and wanted to figure out what Adam's **Number** is. Adam ran the numbers and said he could go and buy that dream home and live the life he wanted if he could earn $300,000. So I set him a goal and he kicked off a three-year challenge to see what could be done.

Three years on and Adam is now making $6,000 a week ($312,000 per annum) by hiring out his crane to other operators. He still operates the crane a few days a week for additional income. See this huge difference, triple the income with half the work! So most of the time Adam is earning money, he's not actually working. He's jumped across the side from employee to self-employed and makes money in his sleep.

Additionally, the extra income Adam has earned enabled him to buy a better home than he originally was going to purchase and now he is in the process of purchasing two more cranes that will provide him an additional $10,000 a week ($936,000) in income before expenses, without an hour extra of work required.

What do you think Adam's revised response to the following question would be:

At some point in the future will your current line of work or business provide you with the opportunity to earn the income that you desire whilst living the lifestyle that you want?
Absolutely!

Do you see the huge shift and difference this has made to Adam's life, by simply stopping to understand what he wanted, knowing his number, making a calculated decision and putting in the work?

This is one of a thousand examples I could give you where people have taken the time to understand what they want and made the decision to go after it – you can too!

It doesn't always have to be huge changes like quitting your job or starting a business Sometimes it can be just looking at your current situation differently. For example, let's say you're an account executive selling Software, but you're stressing yourself out so much you want to quit. Then, you realise that you actually love your company and what you do but you're just putting too much pressure on yourself. You decide you need an alternate source of income, so you train and educate yourself in the property market and build up a cash flow positive property portfolio to earn additional revenue. This additional revenue takes the stress of your day job away and makes it more sustainable, plus, you now have an interest outside of work.

You need to go back to the number exercise, find **Your Number**, look at how you want to design your life, cross-check this with your career projection and make an honest assessment on whether your current career will provide you with the income you need and give you that energy to embrace everyday!

Career Principle 4 – Your work suits your lifestyle

We only get one life so why not design it the way you want it. We spend half of our life at work, so let's make it as enjoyable as possible.

I've personally run profitable companies that I hated and didn't line up with my lifestyle, so I sold them and pursued other things that suited me better. Even though the business was making money, it wasn't making me happy and I couldn't find a way to make it suit my lifestyle so it had to go. When looking at designing a perfect career, you need to formulate a game plan and structure your working week. The objective is to structure your week so not only are you effective and have the time to get the job done but in a way where you also are structuring your lifestyle and ensuring that every week you have allocated enough time for family, health, fun and giving back.

To summarise this chapter, apart from what you do for work, which we have already covered, the following factors will also make a huge difference in the quality and success of your career:

Who do you work with?

The people you work with make a huge difference to the overall happiness and quality of your work. We have all been in good teams and bad teams and the differences are noticeable. Be it self-employed or as an employee, you should try and respectfully move towards working only with people who motivate you, inspire you and make you laugh daily.

Life is way too short to work with people who zap your energy with their negativity. Referring back to the three-year push, if you have negative and lazy people in your team, that's on you, it's because you haven't pushed yourself hard enough to successfully break away from that pack and advance to the next level. What you will notice in every organisation is that the higher you go, the fewer idiots there are. You will start to notice that as you climb the ranks the people around you are more motivated, energetic and overall happier people – these are the people you need to be surrounding yourself with.

What clients do you work with?

You need to know your ideal clients and niche; life is way too short to work with people you don't like. Of course, life isn't perfect and there are economic results that need to be achieved, however, you need to try and become expert enough so you have a reputation which grants you the ability to choose the customers you work with. You need to develop a healthy amount of confidence to say no to the annoying, needy and stressful clients and focus on obtaining quality clients. When you make this paradigm shift, what happens is the law of attraction starts to kick in. You will start attracting a certain type of client that is very similar to your existing clients. If you can find enjoyment in your work and overtime structure and continue to over-deliver to a client base with high-quality people who value your work, you will find a significant increase in not only enjoyment of work, but in the income you receive.

How many hours do you work a week?

There is no one size fits all answer for this, however, what I do highly recommend is knowing exactly what you need to accomplish in any given week to make enough money to live your perfect life-style. Every single one of us is unique, remembering the dreaded income trap, it's important for you to first recognize how much you need to earn, what that's going to take, and then structure your workweek accordingly. Try not to waste too many hours.

Don't take meetings for the sake of it. Every hour you waste on a meaningless meeting is an hour that you're not spending with your partner, your children,or an hour that you could be exercising and doing something fun.

Exercise – I want you to conduct a self-audit and have a think about your past four weeks at work. Go back through your calendar or diary and have a look at how many unnecessary hours you burnt that could have been better spent elsewhere. I guarantee there were at least five hours in your last week you wasted meeting with someone you didn't need to, scrolling through Facebook or Instagram or just hanging out at work. Now imagine that instead, you spent those five hours in a more positive way to increase your overall life *balance* – such as exercising or hanging out with family and friends.

The point to make is that too many of us hang out at work, the gold medal doesn't go to the person who clocks the most hours, it goes to the person who gets the best results, ideally, in the shortest amount of time. Once again, managers don't care how long it takes you to do something, they just want outcomes. People I coach complain that they never get to see their kids or that they're working too late, but they take an hour lunch break to eat a sandwich …

Of course, if you are in a physical role you need to stop and rest and I take my hat off to anyone who does physical labour for a job because it is hard going, but for people in office jobs taking an hour lunch break, something's got to give.

Let's look at an example of how wildly different two people working in the same job can be when it comes to efficiency.

Example

Okay so we have two people Mitch who is Mr Sloppy and Craig who's got his shit together. Let's say they are both mid-40's and have three children.

They are both local area Sales Managers in a national plumbing supply company.

Their job entails each managing five company stores in their areas, making sure that the sales of each store are constantly reaching targets and ensuring that the stores are safe, well-stocked, well managed and profitable.

Starting with Mitch (Mr Sloppy). He's a cruisy bloke, wakes up about 7am, mucks around in the morning, gets ready and heads to his office he usually arrives about 830am, grabs a coffee until about 9am and then jumps straight on the emails, mucks around with the office boys, puts out a few fires, spends up until noon going back and forth on email. At 12pm, heads out to lunch for an hour, then goes and catches up with one of his stores to see what's going on. Because it's the middle of the day when he is visiting the store, he misses loads of calls and his inbox is being flooded with the general corporate junk we all deal with. After the store visit, he gets back to the office about 3pm and spends the next two hours catching up on emails and returning calls. He usually wraps up his day by about 530pm and is home half an hour later. By this time his kids are usually getting ready for dinner, bathing, and bed – meaning he has missed out on a huge opportunity to spend some quality time with his boys. Also, his stores are doing okay, but he's only being reactive and handling issues as they come up. Also, there is no time for Mitch, he hasn't worked on himself, exercised, or done anything towards growing. Essentially, in a year, his life and income will be where it is today.

Now let's have a look at Craig (has his shit together) …

Craig starts his day at 530am heads straight to the gym for a 30 min workout and then kicks off his working day at 7am having a 45-minute coffee meeting with one of his five stores every day of the week. He spends an hour going through their processes, sales figures, stock levels, identifying key customer trends and looking for ways of constant improvement. He is usually back in the office by 830am and he gets on top of his emails and follows up on all calls and reconfirms all of his appointments for the next few days. He has a working lunch and spends the afternoon in constructive meetings and working on plans for the growth of his stores. He generally leaves the office by 3pm, is home by 330pm and spends a few quality hours with his boys and wife.

See a huge difference, same job and life circumstance but Craig has decided to take a conscious look at his working arrangements and structure his week for ultimate *balance* with the benefits being:

Work/Career -His positive approach, commitment, and consistency to his work will no doubt lead to future opportunities and growth within his organisation.

Finance – The above growth in his company will lead to more income and allow his family to grow their wealth, creating the opportunity for amazing experiences with his family.

Family – He gets two to three hours extra a day with his kids, this time is priceless.

Health – By finding the time to consistently exercise, Craig stays in shape and has the energy to be at the very top of his game both at work and at home.

Getting your life into *balance* can be done with a few tiny tweaks. It's so simple, you just need to take the time to sit back and step out of your life, look at it like it's a movie and reconstruct it. It sounds weird, but trust me it works. Sit back, close your eyes and watch your workday and week play out as if you were a director in a movie. Cut out the bits you don't like, add in stuff you think it needs and reconstruct the week making sure that you add in all the key ingredients for balance.

The next step is to go back and implement your new ideal week. It will take about a month to get used to it, but once you have been working smarter and more efficiently for between four to six weeks you will start to notice a huge difference in the key areas of your life.

Now to finalise this chapter and to give you a game plan to follow. First, know your starting point and have faith in knowing you are going to get where you need to be. The only way to earn more money is to do more than what you are paid to do.

Exercise

The only thing standing between where you are today and the life you want tomorrow is your vision.

Now that we have gone through and looked at your natural skill-sets, taken some time to understand your values and what is going to make you happy in your work – I want you to create the vision.

I want you to lay down in a dark room with no distractions and spend 5–10 minutes constructing a new working life and I want you to picture yourself in the exact working arrangements that you would desire. Don't short-change yourself. In this chapter, go big and go into detail. I want you to visualise everything, what you are wearing, the people you are with, where you are working, even checking your internet banking and seeing the income you desire being deposited into your account every week. If this doesn't make you start to smile and get pumped up, I want you to start again and keep revising the version until you create a vision that is so compelling and gets you so excited that it forces you to make the changes needed. Then, I want you to spend literally one minute before you go to bed every night and again in the morning when you first wake up, simply lying there, eyes closed focusing on this vision. The simplicity of doing this will create an imprint in your mind and what this does is forces you to take action to materialise the vision.

Before moving on to the next chapter I want to give you some tools and an action plan to make the necessary changes you need to start living your best working life.

Action Plan

What steps do you need to start taking to move from where you are now to where you need to be? The simplest way to do this is to make a list of action items with specific due dates and start ticking them off one by one. An action plan for an *intrapreneur (employee)* versus an *entrepreneur (self-employed person)* will be different and unique to you but it's important that regardless of your line of work that you:

1. Create a strong and exciting vision
2. Take some time to understand your personality traits and get a good understanding of your key values, ensuring you're in the right line of work. If not, start mapping out a plan to make the necessary changes to move in the right direction.
3. Take some time to understand your skillsets and ensure that your current or future line of work is in sync with your natural strengths.

Lastly, make sure that when you are looking at all the above you keep asking yourself the below question:

At some point in the future will your current line of work or business provide you with the opportunity to earn the income that you desire whilst living the lifestyle that you want?

Treat this question like your north star, if ever you get stuck and are unsure about your career, refer back to this and constantly check in to make sure that what you are doing is going to get you to where you want and need to be. I hope this chapter has given you the courage and motivation to make the necessary changes required from you to go from where you are now and move towards an amazing work/life *balance* full of happiness and an abundance of income.

STEP 4 IN THE PROCESS

BUILDING WEALTH AND GIVING BACK

Building wealth is the key to building a great lifestyle. It's pointless putting all that hard work into growing a great business or career if you have no strategy on how to manage the money you make.

Hopefully, by now you have:

- ▸▸ Implemented a regular exercise plan and a good diet to maximise your energy and what you can achieve each day; and
- ▸▸ You have a great understanding of what **Your Number** is and what you need to earn to live your desired lifestyle;
- ▸▸ You have clarity about your career and how your values and skillsets are aligned to the work you're doing.

Now it's time to talk about what you are going to do with all the money you are about to make. The aim is to be smart with your money, so that one day when you don't want to work – or are unable to work – you don't have to.

I love talking about money and I'm about to show you how you can quickly get your finances into shape and make sure they stay like that forever. The difference between becoming wealthy or staying poor is usually only five or six good or bad financial decisions throughout your lifetime.

One of my previous businesses was a financial planning business where for almost 10 years I helped people grow their wealth and change their lives. I have seen everything and been lucky enough to work with people on all levels of the wealth spectrum. I've helped people with huge amounts of debt completely turn their financial situation around and build an investment portfolio that changed the quality of their life. I've helped thousands of people buy a home, plan to pay off their homes, and build wealth throughout. I've helped people to get back on their feet and prosper after a bankruptcy and a divorce. I've helped the extremely wealthy become even wealthier, helping them manage taxes effectively and structure their financial affairs for maximum gain. Regardless of whether you currently have crippling debts, some savings or are already successful with huge amounts of savings, my money principles are the same. They will help you get to the exact financial position you want to be in.

It makes me incredibly happy when I can show someone a financial strategy that's going to change the course of their financial future. I can physically see the weight of the world comes off their shoulders when for the first time in their life, they know they are going to be okay financially.

Managing Money Like a Boss

Now that you have a good idea of what you want, I'm going to give you two quick hacks that you can easily use to manage and grow your wealth.

Hack #1   Set up money buckets

When you are mapping out your financial future, I want you to start by thinking about what areas make you the happiest. I use a method called *money buckets*. This method is not unique to me and has been a tried and tested way of managing money. We have so many areas of our life that we can spend money on. So I want you to make a conscious decision to spend more money in areas that make you happiest. For example, I essentially spend money in the following areas:

- ▸▸ Travel
- ▸▸ Fun
- ▸▸ Home (mortgage, groceries, clothes, wine, beer, etc)
- ▸▸ Convenience
- ▸▸ Investing

Like everyone, I have a certain amount of money available each week, so I consciously decide how much to fill each bucket to best suit my lifestyle. My bucket system looks like this:

- ▸▸ Travel – full
- ▸▸ Fun – three-quarters full
- ▸▸ Home – half full
- ▸▸ Convenience – full
- ▸▸ Investing – almost full

MONEY BUCKETS

| TRAVEL | FUN | HOME | CONENIENCE | INVESTING |
| FULL | 3/4 FULL | HALF FULL | FULL | FULL |

We love to travel – it's our number one thing. We have plans to circle the globe with our two girls and when we travel we splurge to do it the exact way we want to. We spend money on flying comfortably, staying in amazing places and buying the most amazing experiences. For me, being on holiday means I'm with my family and having the opportunity to enjoy amazing experiences. This makes me the happiest man in the world, so the **travel bucket** gets allocated a lot of cash.

Another bucket that gets allocated a lot of cash is my **convenience bucket**. I'm more than happy to pay people to clean my house, do my gardens, wash my car, cook and do anything else that buys me time. My work commitments drag me away from my family more than I'd like, so when I'm with my girls I'd prefer not to chew up that time doing chores.

I allocate a lot of my cash to my **fun bucket**. I would encourage you to do what I do and write up, or at least have a think about, your 'fun bucket list,' then find the time to make plans to do these things. That way, this bucket is always full and will always have enough money in it to take advantage of cool and exciting opportunities that pop up.

We also try to allocate as much as we can to our **investing bucket**, as we know the more we put away today, the less we will have to work down the track.

You will also notice that my **home bucket** isn't super full. We have a beautiful home, nice cars and nice clothes but, we will always prioritise our travel, convenience and fun buckets over paying off a massive mortgage to live in a mega-mansion we don't need.

This exercise is really important because it gets your life structure in balance and helps you stay focused on what's important in life. I have friends who love cars and aren't fussed about travelling, so I encourage them to fill up their car buckets and go for it. Vice versa, I have friends who live in mansions but wear $10 T-shirts and don't like travelling. We are all different and have different things that excite us.

What I want you to avoid is having your buckets out of balance. Many times over the years I've seen people who put way too much in their home bucket, then there's no money left over for convenience, travel or fun. What ends up happening is that they start to become unhappy, because even though they have an amazing home, they can't afford to pay for someone to look after it. So they spend too much of their own time on maintenance, or are so burdened by mortgage repayments there's no money left over for travel or fun.

Spend some time now and think about how you could consciously decide where to place your money. When you start to develop a financial plan, either personally or with an adviser, make sure you focus on how much money needs to be in specific buckets to ensure you're living your best life.

Hack #2   Get expert advice

When it comes to managing money, you can either get professional advice or go down the 'do it yourself' path. There's no right or wrong, but the key is building a financial plan and having accountability towards it.

I have a financial adviser, Ryan who owns Catalyst Wealth, Ryan manages my family's wealth and my accountant, Mike who owns

Sandford Accounting, manages all of my tax and business affairs. Ryan and Mike are two of the smartest people I know and having these experts in my corner helps me sleep well at night.

I'm a huge fan of outsourcing the important stuff, like wealth creation and finance. This is not the area of your life to go cheap on – find the best people you can afford and pay them what they deserve. Whatever you spend on quality professional advice, you will get back ten times.

Another important reason to have experts in your corner is for the accountability they provide. Ryan, my adviser, knows my goals and checks in on me every quarter to make sure that I'm on track. If I have fallen off the path by spending too much and not investing enough, he will let me know and bring me back into line. I love this about him. I could certainly do it myself, but I value my time highly. I'm not willing to spend time managing the finances when I can pay someone I trust to do this for me and I get the added benefit of the accountability this provides.

Now for a little disclaimer. There are many amazing wealth managers in the world who do a great job and have amazing intentions but … there are also plenty of sharks out there circling who will tell you everything you want to hear and scam you out of your money. My best advice for selecting a financial adviser, if you decide to go down this path, is to simply ask your network of family, friends and work colleagues who they use and trust. There's no better testimonial than an existing client. If you don't know of anyone, then make sure that when meeting an adviser for the first time, you request to speak to at least three existing customers who work with the adviser, to ensure they are competent and trustworthy.

Alternatively, if you have the time, energy, and interest, you can manage your own money and wealth. I'm going to show you the five key areas you need to know for effective wealth management and talk you through each one, step by step. If you have already decided to outsource, please continue to read through to the end of this chapter. Even if you aren't managing your own money directly, you need to have a really solid knowledge of what your adviser is doing with your finances.

Managing Your Own Money and Wealth

When managing your own money and wealth, these are the five areas where you need to have a solid understanding:

1. Debt management
2. Budgeting and saving money
3. Investing money
4. Retirement planning
5. Setting up your children by leaving a legacy

If you can have all these five areas of your finances working well together, then it's not a question of **if** you will be wealthy, it's **when you will be wealthy**.

1. Debt management

To become wealthy, you need to develop a healthy relationship with debt. Debt is like a spouse: if you have a bad relationship with debt, then life's tough; if you have a good relationship with debt, life will be a breeze. You can't become wealthy without debt, so if we're going to have it let's do it right.

It's very simple, the golden rule is to only go into debt (borrow money) to buy something that is going to go up in value or is a tax deduction for business purposes. Most commonly, money is borrowed to buy the following assets:

➤➤ your home
➤➤ investment property
➤➤ a business
➤➤ shares

Referring back to your goals, it's more than likely that you will need to borrow money to get where you want to be financially. This is where I believe it's important to obtain professional financial advice on the best possible lending options that are not only safe but tax-effective and affordable.

Using debt effectively means borrowing money to buy things that go up in value. We've gone through this in my Game Plan but let me give you another slightly more detailed example of how to go about this. Let's say you want to create wealth through property. If you borrowed $500,000 to buy an investment property and the interest on that loan was 4 per cent a year, then here is how the numbers could look:

Bank Interest: $500,000 loan x 4 per cent interest = $20,000 per year
Other costs and taxes: $5,000 per year
Total Outlay: $25,000
Rent Received: $15,000
Out of Pocket Expense: $10,000 per year

So this investment is going to cost you $10,000 a year to hold this property. So, let's fast forward 10 years, you have paid $10,000 a year for 10 years so a total of $100,000 in costs.

But let's say the property you purchased 10 years ago for $500,000 is now worth $800,000. The property has made you $300,000 less your $100,000 costs, so you are $200,000 ahead (before tax). Therefore, you have effectively accumulated $200,000. It's not magic, it's just an effective use of debt.

That's how wealthy people use debt. They borrow money to buy assets such as property, businesses and shares that appreciate in value and multiply their capital, while tenants or dividends pay the majority of the loan expenses. They then leverage off increased capital in one investment to acquire another investment and repeat the process over and over, until they have accumulated enough wealth to live their desired lifestyle.

I've just helped a friend to structure a deal where he borrowed $300,000 to buy a gym franchise. The interest payments on the business loan are $2,700 per month but he is bringing in $12,500 per month after costs and taxes so he's almost +$10,000 a month, I would consider this an effective use of debt.

Now, of course, not every property and investment vehicle has a guaranteed return. That's why it is important to get professional advice and conduct research before borrowing money to invest. To circle back, it's almost impossible to become wealthy without debt, so the importance of having a good relationship with debt is critical to your long-term wealth creation.

Below is a debt schedule, this tool is designed to:

1. Help you understand what your debts are.
2. Identify what debts you can quickly eliminate, reduce or get a better deal.
3. Work out a plan to get rid of "bad debts".

Spend some time now and work through the schedule to get an exact understanding of your current debt position and determine if there is a way for you to reduce or eliminate some of your existing debts:

DEBT	AMOUNT	INTEREST RATE	REPAYMENT	REQUESTED DISCOUNT	GOOD OR BAD DEBT	KEEP OR GET RID OF
MORTGAGE	$ $200,000	3.5%	$2,951	YES	GOOD	KEEP
CREDIT CARD	$ 3,000	16%	$181	YES	BAD	GET RID OF
	$					
	$					
	$					
	$					
	$					
	$					
	$					
	$					
	$					
	$					
	$					
	$					
	$					
	$					
	$					

You can access this template in the bonus workbook section at the back of this book and if you need help completing this, there is also a video tutorial that can be found at tonycaine.com

2. Budgeting and saving money

Before we move on in the exciting world of investing and making money, I want to spend some time talking about budgeting. Budgeting is also the key to knowing **The Number**. In previous chapters, we went through the importance of knowing what your current budget is as well as your desired budget.

Just as you wouldn't walk into the woods without a map, you shouldn't wade through life without a budget. The simplest of budgets can make all the difference between becoming wealthy or not.

If you haven't already identified your number in the previous chapters, take 20 minutes to go back and complete the budget to work out **Your Number**.

When completing your budget, the result will either be:

1. You are in surplus – you spend less than you earn.
2. You are in deficit – you spend more than you earn.

Once you have identified whether you are in surplus or deficit, I want you to be aggressive in reducing every single possible cost – call all of your providers and negotiate a discount on phone plans, electricity, insurance, TV subscriptions, etc. Once you have gone through every expense then do it again and again – strip out every unnecessary expense, until you have the bare minimum expenses. If you are not in surplus, you need to get back to surplus ASAP, as every dollar of surplus can be used to pay off debt or to invest, which is ultimately going to grow your wealth more quickly.

Cash is king. Everybody should have cash at the call to fall back on if something doesn't go to plan, or in case an opportunity of a lifetime pops up. Some of the most successful people I work with have simply been in the right position at the right time with money available to take advantage of an unexpected opportunity.

When it comes to saving, as a general rule of thumb, you need to aim to save a minimum of 10 per cent of your income/profits. This needs to be an automatic payment that gets paid into a separate account as soon as you get paid. For example, if you take home $1,500 per week, you should look at setting up an automatic payment of a minimum of $150 (10 per cent) into a separate savings account. I'll show you how to automate this all shortly.

I recommend you have the following two special accounts:

▸▸ **Emergency Fund**: Everyone should have some savings available for those annoying random things that cost money, like car repair, kids braces, etc. This account should be an online savings account that isn't linked to an ATM card.

▸▸ **Opportunity Fund**: Once you have saved a minimum of $10,000 to cover emergencies, it's a great idea to look at setting up a separate 'opportunity fund'. It's critically important to always have cash available. While I'm writing this, we are right in the middle of COVID-19. This opportunity fund may be either saving your ass right now or can be used to capitalise on the endless investment opportunities that are currently available.

Now here are some options for what to do with the money you have accumulated in savings.

3. Investing money

Here is the fun part. It doesn't matter whether your preference is property, shares, business or your personal development. The goal needs to be to accumulate enough in investments so you don't need to work or can *choose* the work you would like to do.

This book is not meant to be an investment book and I strongly recommend that you seek your own advice. I have been fortunate to spend a decade of my life helping thousands of people structure their finances, but please keep in mind the advice that follows is of a general nature and should not be considered personal advice.

I created this simple stupid drawing to illustrate how to **set up a cash flow system**. Over the years, this system has helped hundreds of my clients become millionaires.

Cash Flow System Example:

This is how the system works. All income (wages, profit, rent, dividends) goes into a central account. This can be an offset account if you have a mortgage. Then all payments are set up to automatically come out of this account.

You start with having a cash hub where all the income is received.

Step 1: You automatically transfer out your mortgage/rent. Try to keep at a max of 35 per cent of your take-home income.

Step 2: You transfer an amount to cover all your bills to a separate account. This should be a max of 25 per cent of income. Then you set up for the bills to come out of this account

Step 3: You allocate an amount for savings, ideally 10 per cent of income. This goes into a separate account.

Step 4: You put money away for investing, ideally 10 per cent of income.

Steps 5/6: You transfer specific amounts to each person in the household for everyday spending. Ideally no more than 10% of income. So if there were two people in the household 5 per cent each. So for example, if the total

take-home figure is $2,000 a week combined. Each
partner in the household would get 5 per cent of this
or $100 each.

Step 7: You allocate some money for travel and fun experiences, ideally 10 per cent.

Example:

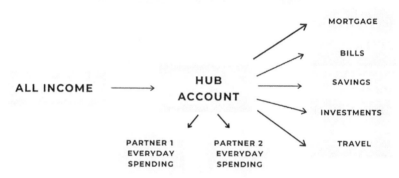

ACCOUNT STRUCTURING

THE BELOW IS FULLY AUTOMATED

ALL INCOME ⟶ HUB ACCOUNT ⟶ MORTGAGE / BILLS / SAVINGS / INVESTMENTS / TRAVEL / PARTNER 1 EVERYDAY SPENDING / PARTNER 2 EVERYDAY SPENDING

I know this seems oversimplified, but it's extremely effective. The
best part is, if you set it up correctly it's all automated and you
never need to worry about it.

Managing money effectively can be boring, but it's worth it.
Out of all the people I've worked with, 99.9 per cent of them want
two things:

▸▸ a nice home debt-free; and
▸▸ enough money so they can live the lifestyle they want.

The only way to achieve this is to be disciplined and install a cash flow system. Start by paying down debt, then start investing as much as you possibly can.

Investing

Tony's Life & Finance Game Plan:

Remember at the very start of this book I was talking about looking after yourself and living longer? So that really comes back into play here. So many people rush big financial decisions because they feel that they are behind and need to "catch up".

The plan I'm about to show you isn't "my opinion", it's more a summarised review of what I've seen and helped thousands of clients of mine do to become both successful in life but also extremely wealthy.

Sorry dude's before we get to that my lawyers need me to read you this:

The information in this book is for general information only. It should not be taken as constituting professional advice. I am not currently a financial adviser. You should consider seeking independent legal, financial, taxation or other advice to check how the information in this book relates to your unique circumstances. I'm not liable for any loss caused, whether due to negligence or otherwise arising from the use of, or reliance on, the information provided directly or indirectly, by use of this book.

Back to the fun stuff. Now there are thousands of ways to build wealth and be comfortable, but here is what I have seen to be most effective. Once again, this is not advice, just a summary of what I have seen work well time and time again:

Step 1 – Invest in yourself first

Successful and wealthy people have invested in themselves first and foremost. You will never find a better investment vehicle than yourself to generate high returns. You need to educate or train yourself with a unique skill that helps you excel in your career or start a great business. This is the quickest way to grow your income.

Step 2 – Start Investing

The income you are generating from your work needs to be invested ASAP. Once again this might not suit everyone's situation depending on your location, career path or personality but the investment path I personally have adopted and have seen work consistently for others is outlined below:

Please remember the numbers below are not specific to your individual circumstance and you should seek your own independent advice.

1. **First Property – 10 per cent:** The aim here is to save hard for at least a 10 per cent down payment on her first property. Let's say you save up $50,000 and spend $500,000 on your first property, you will have a loan of $450,000 (maybe more depending on fees and taxes where you live). This can be an investment, it doesn't have to be your forever home. Please promise me though you will conduct thorough research and buy the best possible property in the location you can afford. DON'T speculate on a maybe location with the next mining boom blah blah blah.
2. **Debt Reduction:** Use your income to pay down this loan as quick as possible and let the property grow.

3. **Avoid the Wedge Property:** Okay, if you've followed along this far hopefully by now you have a property and have created some decent equity but life is changing, you may be moving for work, partnering up, having kids or all of the above. What most people do here is where it all goes wrong. Don't fall into the "I cant rent trap'. Let's say you have your first property from step one, if you have a partner, hopefully they have read this book as well and are also bringing a property to the equation. Now you need a bigger house but can't afford exactly what you want. Lets say what you would want costs $1,500,000 but what you can afford is $1,000,000. It's tempting to buy the $1,000,000 home but I would say mathematically you are better off renting the home you need and keeping the investment you have and continue to rapidly pay down the debt until you can afford to buy the actual home you need. Putting some numbers around this – stay with me I know this is getting a bit mathy, but I'll wrap it up soon . So you have your first property, you're renting a home that suits you, the time when you know you can and should upgrade is when you can afford at least a 20 per cent deposit on your next home. So let's say you've been renting for five years and the home you want and need is now worth $2,400,000. But remember that pesky initial investment we bought almost 10 years ago, well that's now worth $900,000 and you only owe $200,000 so you sell it and you have $700,000 in cash for the next home.

4. **2nd Property:** So your career is going well or your business is growing, your income has increased and

you now have $700,000 to invest in a $2,400,000 property, after costs your loan will be $1,800,000 (approximate). Pat on the back for you, you're nailing it.

5. **Debt Reduction 50% rule:** Okay you're locked in, you're all in now, you've got a pretty decent mortgage the question I get asked all the time is what's next, when do I invest in shares or buy an investment property? The answer is really simple, you have to pass two tests:

   – *Test 1 – Equity:* When you own at least 50 per cent of your home. So let's say this house you bought for $2,400,000 is now worth $3,000,000 and your mortgage is $1,500,000. I don't care how long this takes, don't rush just keep paying down your mortgage and ride it out and wait! Remember there's no rush!

   – *Test 2 – Income:* When you are comfortably handling your mortgage, you have plenty of surplus cashflow to live the life the exact way you want and you have been investing 10 per cent of your income into a savings fund for a minimum of 12 months and haven't noticed you've missed the money then you can start investing.

   This first Investment is what I call the debt reducer investment. What does this mean? This investment's job is to grow in value so you can one day use the growth of this investment to pay off all of your debt. Let's say we go out and buy an investment for $750,000 and borrow the same amount of $750,000 using equity (if this is confusing I'll explain more in pages to come + I have lots of videos in relation to this which can be found at tonycaine.com).

6. **Work Towards becoming Debt Free:** So now we have our home worth $3,000,000 and we owe $1,500,000 +

an investment worth $750,000 that we owe $750,000 on. Let's just chill for 10 years and let this play out. Here is how it may turn out:

10 Years on:

Property	Value	Debt	Equity
Home	$5,000,000	$750,000	$4,200,000
Investment	$1,500,000	$750,000	$750,000

See now if you sold the investment property you could be debt freeeee!

7. **Cruise to The finish Line:** If you've gotten this far, it's very difficult to stuff things up from here. If you haven't already it's imperative that you get professional advice. At this point in life, it's really simple – all you need to do is use a combination of your equity in your home + your retirement savings to invest wisely and buy quality shares and property that are going to generate your income for life.

As you can see, although overly simplified and before the maths whiz's out there get their calculators out and try to analyse my numbers to the 10th decimal point, this wasn't meant to be a detailed financial plan, more a summary to show you how I've seen thousands of successful people do it and how five to six really good financial decisions is all it takes to become really wealthy.

To get technically if you have followed the right path and are actually ready to invest, I have illustrated how I break down where my money is invested. I try to invest 20 – 40 per cent of my income, and here's how I allocate that amount of money:

My Allocation:

- 15 per cent stocks and managed funds (this may seem low but my retirement savings are 100 per cent in stocks so I'm cool to have this figure lower with my personal money).
- 45 per cent property and real estate
- 20 per cent a bond for my kids
- 20 per cent in myself

The stocks and managed funds are all invested in either low-cost exchange-traded funds, listed investment companies or directly into individual stocks. I love the idea of owning great quality companies for the long term. I am obsessed with ETF's. Head to tonycaine. com to learn more but it's as simple as this: Picture there is a huge apple tree and all of the apples on the tree is a stock which is a short description of a company you could invest in. So you can get a ladder or climb up the tree and pick your own stocks, maybe you will get lucky with a few, maybe a few might be rotten or even worse maybe you have a friend or colleague yelling at you from the ground saying "pick that one". That's not an ETF that's a "DIY" approach and unless you have extensive experience in financial markets almost never works. An ETF is like paying the apple farmer who knows every single apple on this tree inside out a small fee to go up there and pick you the best, most ripe apples available. Basically outsource this to the pros!

I also invest a large part of my income in real estate. I like property and I borrow to invest in property where I live, in Sydney, Australia. All the interest on the loan repayments is tax-deductible.

So, by investing in property, I save considerable amounts of tax and have the added benefit of accumulating wealth through property.

I personally only invest in property with a strategic plan, so the investment property I own all can provide me with a future purpose. It's not just random property selection. When I look to invest, I always make sure it's in a major capital city. I invest in property that provides me with the option to either potentially live there one day or to redevelop the asset and make a considerable return on my money. That's my strategy and it's always worked well for me.

If you are just getting started and can't borrow and buy property individually, a great way to start is to buy property through a Real Estate Investment Trust (REIT). This enables you to buy into a fund that owns property for a very small initial outlay.

The next thing I allocate my investing capital to is a tax-effective bond in each of my daughter's names. Technically these are education bonds, but they can be used for any purpose. Hopefully, they will want to study; but who knows, they might want to open a tattoo parlour. Whatever it is, this fund will help them at some point in the future.

The last section I allocate 20 per cent of my savings to, is me. I've been very fortunate to start several successful companies; it's just my thing, I love doing it. I love the concept of starting with an idea and then building infrastructure, systems, hiring people and building a business to be sold for a profit. You can do this with a side hustle …

So, let's finalise this section on investing. The simplest way to work out where to put your money – and how much – is to think back to your goals. Once you have a clear set of goals and a strong vision, you can easily work out what needs to go where and how much risk you are prepared to take in certain areas so you can make sure, at some point in the future, you have the right amount of money to live life on your own terms.

4. Retirement planning

The retirement plans that you are about to read are very unique. The reason for this is that I truly hate the concept of retirement. Before you think I'm crazy and throw this book in the bin, here's why.

I spent almost a decade as a financial adviser, helping people get to retirement. Both my clients and I thought that if they could just save and invest enough, they could accumulate enough to never have to work again. Even though we managed to get these people in a position to retire, 90 per cent of them now wish they weren't retired. They sacrificed so much fun in their 40s, 50s, and 60s trying desperately to pay off their mortgages and invest lots of money, so they would have a large enough bucket of money not to have to work.

After reviewing and working with these people over a long period, the overwhelming feedback has been that they wished they had decided to enjoy the ride a bit more and transition into retirement at their own pace.

Investing for retirement is important. You might not have the luxury of being able to work, due to ill health or other reasons. But it's not worth putting your whole life on hold for a day that may never come …

What I have seen the plain and simple retirement goal is this simple:

- ⇥ You have a debt free property in a place where you are comfortable to live.
- ⇥ You have investments that provide you with at least 80 per cent of your pre-retirement income. So if pre-retirement you were earning $100,000, then before you retire you should have investments which generate at least $80,000 (80 per cent) of this income every year. An easy way to calculate this is divide your

annual income by 4 per cent and this should give you the capital you need to retire with. So to generate $80,000 per year you would need $80,000 /4 per cent = $2,000,000

▸▸ You have $100,000 + in a spare fund to help pay for your children and grandchildren's unexpected expenses.

Live for today but plan for tomorrow.

—Anonymous

5. Setting up your children by leaving a legacy

This doesn't need to be for children only. If you don't have children, this information could be relevant for nieces, nephews, charities or anyone close to you. The goal is to leave the world a better place than you found it. My wife and I take this approach to change the course of our family tree and create generational wealth. Our investment philosophy is largely based on acquiring high-quality assets that generate income and cash flow which will continue into perpetuity.

For example, let's assume that by the time you reach age 70 you have accumulated $5,000,000 worth of assets, providing you with an annual income stream of $200,000. Let's assume you live to 95, and by the time you pass away, the value of these assets would be worth $10,000,000, providing $400,000 in income. Then let's say that these assets are held in an investment trust, with the rules being that these assets are never to be sold and are to be retained in the family but all the income generated from the assets is divided evenly among all your children, grandchildren, and your chosen charity and must be used for investment or educational purposes only. By the time you have been dead for 50 years, the assets in the investment trust that you set up would be worth $40,000,000. They would be generating $2,000,000 in annual income which your children, grandchildren and charity can use to buy their own properties, build wealth, and pay for the best possible education. Imagine if your parents or grandparents had done this; what impact would it have had on your life?

Death doesn't usually bring happy thoughts and no one is immortal. However, I find peace in knowing that my wife and I are going to have an eternal impact on our loved ones and the charities that we care about long after we are gone. This is something that I know will provide you with a lot of happiness.

Maximising Your Finances into the Future

As we finalise the chapter on your finances, I just wanted to do a quick recap to ensure that the fundamentals have sunk in and reassure you that life is a long game, so don't stress if you're not where you want to be just yet. Remember:

> *Life is like riding a bicycle. To keep your*
> *balance, you must keep moving.*

> **—Albert Einstein**

The most important message I hope you have taken from this chapter is that there's no rush, you can take this journey on your own path and design it however you like. I would much prefer you spent more time thinking about your career and made sure you were in the right career then your finances. If you are loving your work you will be able to work for much longer meaning that you aren't in as much of a rush to retire. Anything is possible. With the right planning, structure and dedication, you can and will achieve whatever outcome you're chasing. Just put the time in to create a compelling vision, get the structure right, get the right finance professionals in your corner, develop that plan and make sure that no matter what curveballs life throws at you, you stick as closely to it as you can. If you do this, then I promise that one day you will bridge the gap between where you are now and where you want to be – a*nd* you will have the financial capacity to live the exact life you want!

Exercises for Building Wealth

Expenses

Print out the past three months of all your everyday accounts and credit card accounts, then highlight every single non-essential expense. Cancel them immediately and identify all expenses you can save money on.

Know Your Number

Set up a budget and determine if you are in surplus or deficit. Figure out the type of life you want to live and work out Your Number then chase it like a dog with a bone!

Debts

Identify and list out all your debts, then start the process of getting rid of your bad debts.

Weekly Cash Challenge

Select a figure and withdraw this cash out for everyday expenses, then make it last for seven days. For example, take out $200 and make this last for the whole week. If you can get into this habit every week, it will make a huge difference to your long-term wealth creation. You can also do this digitally by removing all but (X) amount from your everyday bank account and making it last the week.

Financial Goals

Spend some time determining your financial goals, how much they are going to cost you and when you would like to achieve them.

To finalise this section, let me be pushy for a second. Please consider engaging a professional to hold your hand and run these numbers for you. You need help to work out a plan. The best part is once you have a professional looking after your money you can then focus on your day-to-day job knowing that in the long run, everything will be okay.

Giving Back

Once you have gotten on top of your finances and have a plan for creating a profitable business, the natural next step is to think about giving back. The more you give, the better you will live.

The universe has a funny way of rewarding generous people. Once you have made the conscious decision that, throughout your life, you are going to dedicate yourself to improving the lives of others, everything changes for you.

Giving is not specific. Giving is taking either your time, your money or your possessions and passing them over to someone who needs them more than you do. I hear a lot of people who tell me that they will give money away to charity 'once they have made it' or 'when they have more time down the track'. The reality is, if you don't give anything away when you're poor, nothing is going to change when you're rich.

There's a fine line here. You do need to look after yourself first, so you are in a position to be able to help others a lot more. My mother is the sweetest lady on the planet, she is completely selfless. I remember one time she was on her way to work and saw a man standing on the side of the road with a cup, begging for money. It was raining quite heavily and the man was getting saturated. Most people would have continued driving, but not mum. She stopped to chat with this person, found out that he was actually blind and asked what she could do for him. He jokingly asked her for an umbrella, so mum got back in her car, drove to the local store, bought an umbrella and gave it to the man. By the time she got to work, she was an hour late because of all of this. She nearly got laid off but she didn't mind; she saw someone who needed help and put herself to the side to help someone else out.

Giving time is as powerful as money. This doesn't have to be charity, there are a thousand ways you can help others just by doing something small. Here are a few examples:

- ▶▶ Cut your elderly neighbour's lawns.
- ▶▶ Pick up groceries for your elderly neighbours.
- ▶▶ Give your seat on the bus to the elderly lady or elderly who needs it more than you do.

There are hundreds of daily events that occur which enable you to do something simple that helps someone else and makes the world a better place.

Give Someone an Opportunity

We all need to catch a break now and then. I have had two great mentors, Harry Moustakas and Troy Phillips. These men saw something in me and gave me an opportunity in a business that made me who I am today. When I met these men I was at a crossroads in my life. They swooped me up, took me into their companies, gave me a place to go every day and showed me not only how to run a successful business and make money but how to be a good person and look after people.

I'm sure anyone reading this with any level of success has caught a break at some time. Someone has given you an opportunity that has helped you get to where you are now. I want you to think about who you can help out; what's something that you could do that could change the course of someone's life? If the whole world made a conscious decision to help one person improve their life, then the world would be a much better place.

What introduction could you make, who could you put someone in touch with, for an opportunity that could change their life?

Do you know someone with amazing talents? If you just lent them the money to get their idea or business off the ground, would that help them become an amazing success?

Is there someone in your life who needs to come and stay at your place for a while, to get away from an abusive relationship?

We all live in a bubble and we don't want it to be popped. We are all guilty of this. It's not ideal when other people eat into our time and muck up our plans with their own dramas. Sometimes you need to realise that others are hurting and be big enough to understand that you have the ability and resources to help. Decide to go out of your way to help a person in need.

Charity Work

I believe everyone should support a cause, something that is close to you. We have all been touched by tragedy and loss. If you're not already working with a charitable organisation regularly, I'd love you to think about which cause means a lot to you and start working with them.

Start small, maybe with a small monthly donation and volunteering once a year. Then build up to doing more volunteering, raising funds and awareness for whatever cause means a lot to you. The selflessness of taking your time and resources and giving them to someone who needs help is the most satisfying thing that you can do with your life. It will do more for your own mental health than anything else.

Please don't skip over this section, as this is the glue that binds everything together. If you have 10/10 success in all other areas of your life and neglect this part of it, there will be a gaping hole that only the act of giving can fill.

There we have it, we have gone through the 4 step process:

▶ **STEP 1**: Generate Energy and Maximise your Health

Maximise the energy you have and maximise what you can accomplish each day.

▶ **STEP 2**: The Number

Understand how much money you need to earn from your career or business, to live the life you desire.

▶ **STEP 3**: Find Balance & Success in your Work

Design a working situation that provides you with the lifestyle and flexibility you desire.

▶ **STEP 4**: Build Wealth & Give Back

Create sustainable wealth and help others along the way.

For the rest of this book, I want to finish off by showing you how you can build structure into your life with an ideal week and also help you find ways to build some fun into it so you can enjoy the ride.

PLANNING YOUR IDEAL WEEK

8

One of the keys to becoming successful and building an amazing lifestyle is routine. Let's face it, there's a lot that we need to fit into every week, so the more organised you are, the better chance you have of succeeding.

I want to help you to construct a perfect working week. Let's put money to the side for a moment and spend five minutes thinking about the following questions:

- ▶▶ *How many hours do you spend every week at work?*
- ▶▶ *How much time are you wasting and what crappy stuff could you eliminate from your week?*
- ▶▶ *What extra skills or education do you need to take you to the next level; how many hours a week do you need to dedicate to these?*
- ▶▶ *Who can you lean on to get some additional support?*
- ▶▶ *What low-value tasks are you still doing that you can either completely stop or hand over to someone else?*

▸ *What are the really important family and personal things you want to build into your week, like watching kids' sports, going out to dinner, exercising, etc?*

Once you've thought about all these important things, the next step is to implement a structure for your ideal week. I have included an example of my ideal week, to give you an idea of how I fit everything in:

MY PLANS FOR THIS WEEK

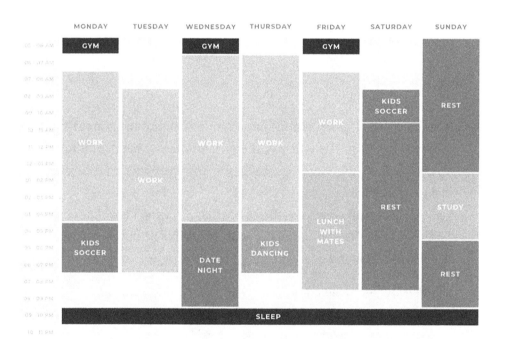

The main thing to point out from my weekly schedule is **consistency**:

▸ I aim to wake up and go to sleep at the same time every day (loosely, I'm not a soldier).
▸ I have clearly defined times allocated for work/family/ exercise/study.

▶▶ I finish work at the same time every day (where possible).

▶▶ I allow consistent time to spend with family and friends.

▶▶ There's not too much weekend work, apart from tidying up, personal development, and study. This allows me to reset for the week ahead.

▶▶ There are gaps for spare time when I call friends and family, stay in touch with people, or go out of my way to give back.

As happens to everyone, things will pop up and throw your week out of whack; things like conferences, unavoidable late meetings, birthdays, funerals, kids' events, anniversaries, deadlines, overseas travel and holidays. However, the key is to try and maintain your ideal week for 70-80 per cent of the year. I have stuck to the ideal week structure for more than a decade now and it certainly does reduce my stress. By living my ideal week, I know that I can tick the boxes that need to be ticked and I'm not missing anything.

As we continue through the book, I want you to refer back to this section and start to design your ideal week that you can use as a reference point.

EXERCISE: Design Your Ideal Week

Pull up a basic spreadsheet or a piece of paper to help plan your ideal week. Aim to block out 30 minutes to sit down and design it, ensuring you have included all the key elements to maintain a balanced life.

I know this exercise may seem academic or simplistic, but I can't emphasise how much it has helped me to stay focused, align with my vision and achieve the goals I set out to accomplish each and every day.

ENJOYING THE RIDE

9

When was the last time you genuinely said to yourself: 'That was unbelievable!' Having fun in life is everything. I hope that after reading through this book, you now have the motivation to change, have clarification on the type of life that you want to live and can find balance in your life. Then while you are doing your best to maximise your success, you are also enjoying the ride.

Most of us are so caught up in the daily grind, we have no idea what we are missing out on and have forgotten how to have fun.

What makes you happy, what are the things that you like to do that make you smile? I'll tell you how to recognise them. Generally, when you are in the middle of them you are not thinking about much else, just focusing on the task at hand. This is what some refer to as **being in your flow**. Studies have shown that the happiest people on the planet are living a **balanced** life, which enables them to experience their **flow** regularly.

Flow doesn't have to cost money or take up a lot of time. I break it up into three categories: daily flow, weekly flow and bucket list flow.

Daily Flow

This is just something simple that you enjoy doing daily. It could be as simple as:

- Getting your daily coffee
- Reading a few pages of a book you're into
- Listening to a podcast
- Going to the gym
- Calling a friend
- Meditating
- Watching your favourite Netflix show

Whatever it is, it's just a small thing that makes you happy each and every day. Treat this as your 'time out' time. This isn't the time when you are trying to formulate your plan for world domination or how you can become a millionaire; this is just an outlet that you can look forward to each day, to take your mind off the general pressures that we all face daily.

Weekly Flow

This is more substantial and something that's not possible for you to do every day. But it's still one of your favourite things to do. So try and aim to do it at least once a week; book it into your schedule and make sure that nothing stops it from occurring. A couple of common examples of this may be:

- Going for a surf
- Baking
- Watching your favourite team play, either live or on TV
- Going to the movies

- ⏩ Playing golf
- ⏩ Taking your kids to the park
- ⏩ Going out to a restaurant
- ⏩ Hiking
- ⏩ Drawing
- ⏩ Sitting down and reading a book for an hour

Whatever your outlet is, it's important to schedule it weekly. I want this to be something for you to look forward to, which will help get you through a shitty week if things aren't going your way.

Bucket List Flow

Finally, everyone needs something big to aim for. It doesn't matter how big or how much this is going to cost. I want you to think of your big-ticket item, something so epic that when you think about actually doing it you get excited. It's so epic that even the thought of it can pull you out of a crappy state of mind and turn your frustration into excitement and motivate you to keep going because you know that if you put the work in you are going to one day be in a position to be able to have this amazing experience.

Last year I went heli-skiing with my wife in New Zealand. The exhilaration of being flown into a mountain and dropped off, then the freedom of snowboarding down a mountain with my wife right beside me on untouched snow in the middle of an amazing place was something that I know we will never forget for as long as we live. Doing this has inspired us to pick out a new amazing adventure to put on the goal sheet and aim for.

Some suggestions to get you thinking could be:

- ⏩ Go to the NFL Super Bowl
- ⏩ Walk the Great Wall of China

- ▸▸ Drive a Ferrari through the Swiss Alps
- ▸▸ Go cage diving with great white sharks
- ▸▸ Watch the PGA Masters at Augusta
- ▸▸ Buy backstage VIP tickets to your favourite artist's concert
- ▸▸ Climb Mount Everest

I want you to go big here and write down at least five amazing experiences. Then go back to the finance section and add these to your financial goals. Aim to do one of these at least every five years.

EXERCISE: Complete Your Flow Chart

To wrap up this chapter, I want you to do this. Don't put all your focus on getting fit or getting rich. Of course, I'm super keen to make sure you achieve your end goal and that all of your hopes and dreams come true, but life is short and sometimes cruel – no one knows when their number is up and it's game over. So get out there and do all the cool stuff you want to do. Don't wait until it's too late!

DAILY FLOW	WEEKLY FLOW	BUCKET LIST FLOW
Walk Dog	Play Golf	Walk the Great wall of China

*template available at **tonycaine.com**

IMPLEMENTING THE GAME PLAN

/10\

Before I let you back into the real world to build an amazing life for you and your family, I want to do a super quick recap. I hope your highlighter has run out of ink and there are dog-ears all over this book that you can refer back to. Treat this book as a life textbook; in times when you are lacking motivation, refer back to your 'why' to remind yourself why you are working so hard.

Let's quickly recap on the journey and look at the key steps that you need to take to live an amazing life full of health, wealth, happiness and fulfilment.

▶ STEP 1. Generate Energy and Maximise your Health

The most important thing about managing our health is the energy that it provides us. The way you look from living a healthy lifestyle is just a bonus. Energy is the key to life; you can't be successful without it and the key to having great energy is health. I want you to be conscious as you are walking around today; notice different people's energy levels and how they're generally going about their day. Watch the body language of people who have good energy, compared to the ones who have bad energy.

Energy creates time; the people who look after their bodies and treat themselves right are winners. Why do you think all the best cars are parked outside the gym at 5am? It's because high performers look after themselves, they have a lot of energy; so they get up earlier than the rest of us and accomplish more in their day; therefore they make more money and are generally more successful.

Remember:

- ▸▸ Good health = energy
- ▸▸ Energy = the ability to be able to get up earlier and accomplish more in a day
- ▸▸ More accomplishments = more income and success
- ▸▸ More income and success = more money
- ▸▸ More money = better lifestyle

Successful people simply have more time. Getting up two hours earlier than anyone else every day creates 10 hours a week, which is 520 extra hours a year. If you divide that by a 40-hour workweek, that's an extra 13 weeks a year of work. That's a quarter of the year extra they get on top of an average year. So next time you look at someone who is doing well in life, before you default to the 'they got lucky' thought, maybe it's just simple maths and they have more time than you!

▸ **STEP 2.** Know The Number

Knowing your number is like having a key to unlock success in your future. Once you know what it is, what you want and what it's going to cost, then you can plan your ideal week to make sure you achieve all of your goals while living a fun and balanced life.

▶ **STEP 3.** Find Balance & Success in your Work

I hope at this point you now understand the importance of making sure your career provides you with:

- ▶▶ a lifestyle that you love;
- ▶▶ the income you desire; and
- ▶▶ inspiration to get to the top of your game.

Remember to constantly ask yourself this question: *At some point in the future, will your current line of work provide you with the opportunity to earn the income that you desire while living the lifestyle that you want?*

The key thing I want you to remember is that it's a long race. Don't let your lack of education, resources, or finances be a hurdle. They may be holding you back right now, but if you have a strong enough vision for the business you want, you will find a way to make it work overtime. Even if you are in a bad place with your business or career at the moment, that's okay – sometimes we have to go to that place to get to where we want to go. Once you do get there, you're going to be so glad you hung in there and made a decision to chase your dreams.

Never think it's too late; remember retirement is something that people who never find their passion do. People who love their work never retire; they continue to do what they love and it creates an amazing lifestyle for them. However long it takes, commit today that you are going to take action to start moving towards a business that you love, which provides you with the exact lifestyle you desire and the income you need.

I want you to focus on this vision every day. Decide that you're no longer going to put up with living a mediocre lifestyle. Promise yourself that you are going to commit to doing whatever is necessary to take you from where you are right now to where you want to be.

Our work and business have such a huge impact on both our happiness and the quality of our lifestyle, so I hope some of the information in here has given you the motivation to go out and chase your dreams.

▸ **STEP 4.** Build Wealth and Give Back

Money makes the world go around. The more you have, the better not only your life will be, but you will have much more impact on the quality of other people's lives. Money isn't the root of all evil; used incorrectly it could be, but if you are smart with your money and put together a plan, then finances become like a machine that is always working for you in the background.

The goal with money and finances is to get to a point where it's no longer an issue. You know you have made it when you don't even need to think about money. You have enough to do what you want to do, day in and day out; you have enough invested to know that you are going to be able to do this for as long as you live. Once you get to this point, the fear of money will have been completely removed. This is where the exciting part comes in – you can use your money to take advantage of exciting opportunities, which in turn will lead to even more money and the ability to help others improve their lives.

Action Plan

Remember that the goal of this book is to get your career and your finances to a point where you no longer have to worry about them and can find a peaceful, fun way to enjoy the rest of your life. Go back and complete the exercises at the end of each chapter, then use this book as a reference tool for the rest of your life.

Down the track, if you begin to notice that some areas are not as strong as others, the best way to fix this is to go back to the end of that chapter, complete the exercise and then make that exercise a part of your life long term.

It's okay to have self-doubt, we all have it. The difference between the ones who succeed and the ones who fail is their belief system. It's okay to not know exactly how you are going to get to where you need to be, but the moment you stop believing you can get there, you will kill the dream that lives inside you.

If you create a vision that is strong enough, continue to believe that you will get to where you need to be and continue to take action every day, the world will start to notice and you will begin to see things start to go your way.

I want you to change your mindset from: *I could never have any of that* to *If I just believe in myself, take action, and work towards my dreams every day, then you never know what could happen.*

I want to thank you for coming on this journey with me. I hope I have helped in a small way to get you excited about a new future, one full of everything you have dreamed of. I'm so excited for you to get out there and start working towards the life of your dreams.

I hope I have convinced you that, regardless of your starting point and what you have or are experiencing, you **can** take action towards changing your life. By creating a compelling vision and by taking action every day to move towards your vision, one day you will wake up in the life of your dreams.

You too can have it all. It's a long race, so I want you to enjoy the journey and not kill yourself along the way. The key is finding the **balance** in everything that you do and trusting the process of knowing that you will get to where you want to be.

Bit by bit, day by day, week by week, year by year, you will begin to notice yourself getting better in every part of life. This becomes addictive and you will want more. That's when the real magic happens – as you begin to notice huge changes in the quality of your life and the impact you are having on the people around you.

There will be times when you think you're not worthy or it's too hard to change. Doubt will creep in and try to get you to go back to your old habits. I hope the words in this book help you to find a way through those tough times and help you to keep pushing towards the life of your dreams.

Thank you so much. I'm so excited for you to see the next level of your life.

Tony Caine

Tony Caine
Founder of tonycaine.com

SYNOPSIS

After starting a career in professional sports, then suddenly having to pivot into the business world after a horrifying injury, In MoneyLife, Tony Caine outlines how to maximise success in life and your career. Tony talks through his 4 Step methodology that has helped him and thousands of others to answer the ultimate question – how can I be happy and successful at the same time …

Based on Tony's real-life experience with much trial and error, Tony outlines his formula to:

- ▸▸ Maximise your energy
- ▸▸ Build a successful career or business
- ▸▸ Grow your wealth and create a legacy
- ▸▸ Design a great lifestyle and enjoy amazing experiences

MoneyLife is a guide that will give you the tools you need to take your life to the next level.

BONUS SECTION

MONEY LIFE TEMPLATES

MODULE
ONE

BUILDING A
FOUNDATION

MODULES

- SELF - ASSESSMENT
- PLANNING YOUR IDEAL WEEK
- FINDING YOUR FLOW

1. SELF ASSESSMENT

INSTRUCTIONS:
Be honest when completing the questions below, as this tool is critical in discovering what areas of your life you need to start working on. I don't want you to share this with anyone; it's just for you, it's a chance for you to be honest with yourself. It's also our starting point for making long-lasting positive changes. Circle the number out of 10 that you believe you are at in the following five key areas. A score of one indicates you're not doing so well right now; a score of 10 means you're doing amazingly well.

HEALTH
How happy are you with the way you look? The amount of sleep you get? The amount of overall energy that you have? Your general mood? Your motivation levels? Circle your overall self-assessment of your health out of 10.

1 2 3 4 5 6 7 8 9 10

FINANCES
Are you living in a house that you love? Do you drive the car you want? Do you have money available to regularly travel and do the things that make you happy? Have you got a financial plan in place, to ensure you continually grow your wealth and will be able to provide for your children's education, your own future, and the generations to come after you? Circle your overall self-assessment out of 10

1 2 3 4 5 6 7 8 9 10

WORK & BUSINESS
Out of 10, how much are you enjoying work? Are you moving towards your career or business goals? Are you in the right business and earning the money you desire? How stressed are you? Circle your overall self-assessment out of 10.

1 2 3 4 5 6 7 8 9 10

HAPPINESS
How often do you spend time doing the things that really make you happy? Would you say you have a fun life? Do you have things to look forward to in life? Circle your overall self-assessment out of 10.

1 2 3 4 5 6 7 8 9 10

GENEROSITY
Are you fulfilled? When was the last time you went out of your way to help someone else? Giving is about changing your mindset to be conscious that other people need help rather than actually wanting to make an effort to make a positive difference in other people's lives on a regular basis. Circle your overall self-assessment of how generous you are out of 10.

1 2 3 4 5 6 7 8 9 10

1. SELF ASSESSMENT SCORE

CURRENT SCORE

Now by adding them together, what's your total life score out of 50 at present?

Health   _____

Finances   _____

Work and Business   _____

Happiness   _____

Generosity   _____

Total   _____ / 50

SUMMARY

If you are at 10/10 in all the areas, then congratulations! If you're like the 99.9 per cent of the rest of us, it's likely that there are areas where you are doing well and areas where you could use some help. The aim of this course is to help you make incremental changes in all parts of your life, which together will culminate in a whole new outlook and amazing life for yourself. The aim is not to be perfect – no one scores 10/10 in all categories all of the time. That would be impossible, and we all go through dark days, weeks, months, and years. By the end of this course, I want to get you to a point where you are at a consistent seven or eight out of 10 in all categories, most of the time.

2. IDEAL WEEK

INSTRUCTIONS:
PREPARING YOUR IDEAL WEEK

The key to becoming successful and building an amazing lifestyle is routine. Let's face it there is a lot that we need to fit into each week so the more routined and organised you are the more chance you have of succeeding. I want to help you to construct a perfect working week.

The following page is a template that will help you to design your ideal week. When completing the below here are a few tips:

1. Aim to wake up and go to sleep at the same time every day.
2. Have clearly defined times allocated for work/family/exercise/ and study.
3. Try and finish work at the same time every day (where possible).
4. It's trial and error. Keep tweaking until you find a routine that works for you.

MY PLANS FOR THIS WEEK

MONDAY	TUESDAY	WEDNESDAY	THURSDAY	FRIDAY	SATURDAY	SUNDAY
GYM		GYM		GYM		REST
WORK	WORK	WORK	WORK	WORK	KIDS SOCCER	
				LUNCH WITH MATES	REST	STUDY
KIDS SOCCER		DATE NIGHT	KIDS DANCING			REST
SLEEP						

IDEAL WEEK- YOUR TURN

IDEAL WEEK

	MONDAY	TUESDAY	WEDNESDAY	THURSDAY	FRIDAY	SATURDAY	SUNDAY
05 - 06 AM							
06 - 07 AM							
07 - 08 AM							
08 - 09 AM							
09 - 10 AM							
10 - 11 AM							
11 - 12 PM							
12 - 01 PM							
01 - 02 PM							
02 - 03 PM							
03 - 04 PM							
04 - 05 PM							
05 - 06 PM							
06 - 07 PM							
07 - 08 PM							
08 - 09 PM							
09 - 10 PM							
10 - 11 PM							

**I HAVE INCLUDED
THESE IN EVERY WEEK**

- ☐ FAMILY TIME
- ☐ 150 MINUTES EXERCISE
- ☐ REGULAR SLEEP
- ☐ WORK
- ☐ MATES/FUN
- ☐ SELF IMPROVEMENT
- ☐ REST/RELAXATION

3. FINDING YOUR FLOW

INSTRUCTIONS:
FINDING YOUR FLOW

When was the last time you genuinely said to yourself: 'That was unbelievable!' Having fun in life is everything. I hope that after going through this course, you will find the motivation to change, have clarification on the type of life that you want to live, and can find balance in your life.

Fill out your flow chart below, and aim to put at least three items in all three columns! Don't be afraid to go big here, we are trying to reignite the flame of life for you here, this is what it's all about!

DAILY FLOW	WEEKLY FLOW	BUCKET LIST FLOW
Walk Dog	Play Golf	Walk the Great wall of China

MODULE
TWO

HEALTH

MODULES

1. MENTAL HEALTH
2. PHYSICAL HEALTH
3. HEALTH OF RELATIONSHIPS

MENTAL HEALTH

4 WEEK MENTAL HEALTH CHALLENGE

1. I WILL AIM TO MEDITATE FOR 10 MINUTES EACH MORNING AND WHEN I DO I WILL:

   ☐ FOCUS ON WHAT IM GRATEFUL FOR

   ☐ VISUALISE MY GOALS & SEE MY FUTURE SUCCESS

   ☐ THINK ABOUT WHO I CAN HELP THAT DAY

2. I WILL PUT MORE FOCUS ON CREATING DEEPER FACE TO FACE PERSONAL CONNECTION WITH PEOPLE

3. STAY ACTIVE

4. FIND A WAY TO RELAX EVERYDAY - FIND 20 MINUTES MINIMUM FOR DAILY FLOW

5. SIGNIFICANTLY MINIMISE SCREEN TIME REPLACE PHONE WITH A BOOK

	MEDITATE DAILY	1 ON 1 CONNECTION	STAY ACTIVE	DAILY FLOW	READ
EXAMPLE	✔	✔	✔	✔	✔
WEEK 1					
WEEK 2					
WEEK 3					
WEEK 4					

EXERCISE

4 WEEK EXERCISE CHALLENGE

CURRENT WEIGHT   -   _____ KG   GOAL WEIGHT   -   _____ KG

1 I WILL AIM TO COMPLETE THE FOLLOWING EXERCISE WEEKLY:

☐ 5 X 30 MIN SESSIONS

☐ 3 X 50 MIN SESSIONS

☐ 6 X 25 MIN SESSIONS

2 I HAVE FOUND A WAY TO EXERCISE WITH SOMEONE ELSE/TEAM ☐

3 I HAVE FOUND EXERCISE I DON'T HATE ☐

4 I KNOW MY LIMITS AND AM PUSHING MYSELF WITHOUT OVER DOING IT ☐

4 I HAVE FOUND A ROUTINE THAT SUIYTS MY LIFESTYLE ☐

	150 MINUTES	TEAM EXERCISE	ENJOYMENT	I KNOW MY LIMIT	ROUTINE
EXAMPLE	✔	✔	✔	✔	✔
WEEK 1					
WEEK 2					
WEEK 3					
WEEK 4					

POST CHALLENGE WEIGHT   -   _____ KG

DIET

4 WEEK DIET CHALLENGE

CURRENT WEIGHT   -   KG   GOAL WEIGHT   -   KG

1   I WILL RESTRICT MY DAILY CALORIE INTAKE TO _____

2   I WILL FAST UNTIL _____ EVERYDAY

3   I WILL RESTRICT MY ALCOHOL INTAKE TO A MAX OF 7 STANDARD DRINKS PER WEEK ☐

4   80% OF MY MEALS WILL BE MADE UP OF   ☐   50% VEGETABLES

         ☐   25% CARBS

         ☐   25% PROTEIN

5   I WILL DRINK 2 LITRES OF WATER PER DAY

	RESTRICTED CALORIES	FASTED	RESTRICTED ALCOHOL	80% RULE	2 LITRES OF WATER
EXAMPLE	✓	✓	✓	✓	✓
WEEK 1					
WEEK 2					
WEEK 3					
WEEK 4					

POST CHALLENGE WEIGHT   -   KG

SLEEP

4 WEEK SLEEP CHALLENGE

① I HAVE DOWNLOADED THE <u>SLEEP JOURNAL</u> ☐

② I WILL GO TO BED AT ____-_____ PM EVERY NIGHT.
    AND WAKE UP AT ____-_____ AM EVERYDAY.

③ I HAVE A COMFORTABLE SLEEP ENVIRONMENT INCLUDING MY BED, LIGHTING
    AND APPROPRIATE HEATING/COOLING ☐

④ I AM BUDGETING ENOUGH TIME FOR 7 -9 HOURS OF SLEEP PER NIGHT
    ☐

⑤ I AM LIMITING ALCOHOL & CAFFEINE CONSUMPTION PRIOR TO BED ☐

	SLEEP JOURNAL	BED TIME	ENVIRONMENT	7 - 9 HOURS	LIMIT STIMULANTS
EXAMPLE	✔	✔	✔	✔	✔
WEEK 1					
WEEK 2					
WEEK 3					
WEEK 4					

REFERENCE:
https://www.sleepfoundation.org/sleep
-diary

RELATIONSHIP HEALTH

KEY RELATIONSHIPS AUDIT

It's your tune to work out the quality of your relationships, the below relationship audit enables you to get a realistic and simplistic view of the quality of your relationships.

The Action Plan after this will help you to work on the next steps you need to take to start improving your overall relationships:

CURRENT RELATIONSHIP SCORE

Spouse _____
Children _____
Family (Parents & Siblings) _____
Friends _____
Colleagues _____
Higher Purpose. _____

Total _____ / 60

RELATIONSHIP AUDIT

1 I WILL COMMIT TO IMPROVING ANY RELATIONSHIP WITH A SCORE LESS <7 ☐

2 I WILL STEP UP AND MAKE FIRST CONTACT TO ANYONE I'M NOT CURRENTLY SPEAKING WITH ☐

3 I WILL MAKE A CONSCIOUS EFFORT EVERYDAY TO IMPROVE THE LIVES OF EVERYONE IN MY CLOSE CIRCLE ☐

4 I WILL REMEMBER THAT MOST PEOPLE ARE JUST DOING THEIR BEST WITH THE TOOLS THEY HAVE ☐

5 I'LL BE THE ONE TO BRING OTHERS TOGETHER ☐

6 I HAVE FOUND A HIGHER PURPOSE TO BELIEVE IN ☐

MODULE THREE

FINANCES

MODULES

1. FINANCIAL GOALS & THE STARTING POINT
2. BUDGETING & THE NUMBER
3. INVESTING
4. RETIREMENT PLANNING
5. LEAVING A LEGACY

YOUR GOALS - Example

NAME OF GOAL	WHEN YOU WANT TO ACHIEVE IT BY?	WHAT IS IT GOING TO COST?
BUY A 3-STORY WATERFRONT HOME IN SMITH STREET	10 YEARS	$ 4M
RETIRE WITH $3,000 PER WEEK	18 YEARS	$ 100K PER YR
FLY BUSINESS CLASS TO PARIS	ANNUALLY	$40,000
STAY AT CONRAD MALDIVES RANGALI ISLAND.	ANNUALLY	$50,000
PAY FOR DAUGHTERS HARVARD EDUCATION	12 YEARS	$300,000
-	-	$ -
-	-	$ -
-	-	$ -
-	-	$ -
-	-	$ -
-	-	$ -
-	-	$ -
-	-	$ -
-	-	$ -
-	-	$ -
-	-	$ -
-	-	$ -
-	-	$ -

FIND YOUR NUMBER

EXPENSE NAME	MONTHLY AMOUNT	UPGRADING Y/N	TOTAL MONTHLY AMOUNT
EXAMPLE MORTGAGE/RENT	*$ 2,000*	*YES / NO*	*$ 4,000*
MORTGAGE/RENT	$ -	YES / NO	$ -
ELECTRICITY/GAS	$ -	YES / NO	$ -
WATER/GARBAGE	$ -	YES / NO	$ -
VEHICLE PAYMENT	$ -	YES / NO	$ -
VEHICLE INSURANCE	$ -	YES / NO	$ -
GAS/TRANSPORT	$ -	YES / NO	$ -
GROCERIES	$ -	YES / NO	$ -
ENTERTAINMENT	$ -	YES / NO	$ -
TELEPHONE	$ -	YES / NO	$ -
CABLE/INTERNET	$ -	YES / NO	$ -
CREDIT CARD	$ -	YES / NO	$ -
LOAN PAYMENT	$ -	YES / NO	$ -
PET	$ -	YES / NO	$ -
PERSONAL	$ -	YES / NO	$ -
MEDICAL	$ -	YES / NO	$ -
OTHER	$ -	YES / NO	$ -

TOTAL $ -   P/M

X 12

EQUALS

HERES YOUR NUMBER ⟶ $ -   P/YR

NET WEALTH- STARTING POINT

ASSETS		LIABILITIES		
ASSET	VALUE	LIABILITY	AMOUNT OWED	REVIEW
	$ -		$ -	☐
	$ -		$	☐
	$ -		$	☐
	$ -		$	☐
	$ -		$ -	☐
	$ -		$ -	☐
	$ -		$ -	☐
	$ -		$ -	☐
	$ -		$ -	☐
	$ -		$ -	☐
	$ -		$ -	☐
	$ -		$ -	☐
	$		$ -	☐
	$ -		$ -	☐
	$ -		$ -	☐
Ⓐ TOTAL	$ -	Ⓑ TOTAL	$ -	

TO CALCULATE YOUR NET WEALTH:

TAKE YOUR TOTAL ASSETS $ -   **LESS TOTAL DEBTS** $ -

Ⓒ **NET WEALTH =** $ -

FINANCES - NEXT STEPS

YOUR NEW NUMBER $ -   P/YR

_____

YOUR CURRENT ANNUAL NET INCOME $ -   P/YR

_____

IS YOUR NEW NUMBER: LESS THAN CURRENT   ☐

MORE THAN CURRENT   ☐

WHAT DOES THIS MEAN?

Now we only have two options: earn more or have less. This is probably going to be one of the most important parts of your life, this decision right now.

INVESTING

 # FIND AN EXPERT!

MONEY BUCKETS

TRAVEL	FUN	HOME	CONENIENCE	INVESTING
FULL	3/4 FULL	HALF FULL	FULL	FULL

ACCOUNT STRUCTURING

THE BELOW IS FULLY AUTOMATED

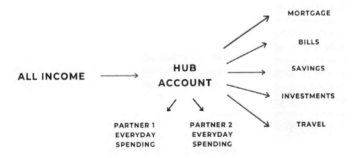

ALL INCOME → HUB ACCOUNT

MORTGAGE
BILLS
SAVINGS
INVESTMENTS
TRAVEL

PARTNER 1 EVERYDAY SPENDING
PARTNER 2 EVERYDAY SPENDING

INVESTING

PROPERTY INVESTING EXAMPLE

Summary	Year 1	Year 5	Year 10	Year 15	Year 20
Property Value	$500,000	$669,113	$895,424	$1,198,279	$1,603,568
Debt	$450,000	$450,000	$450,000	$450,000	$450,000
Net Value	**$50,000**	**$219,000**	**$445,424**	**$748,279**	**$1,153,568**
Rent Recieved	$20,00	$26,765	$35,817	$47,931	$64,143
Annual Interest	$22,500	$22,500	$22,500	$22,500	$22,500
Annual Costs	$5,000	$6,691	$8,954	$11,983	$16,036
Total Costs P/A	-$7,500	-$2,427	$4,363	$13,448	$25,607

MY INVESTMENT PLAN (NOT FINANCIAL ADVICE)

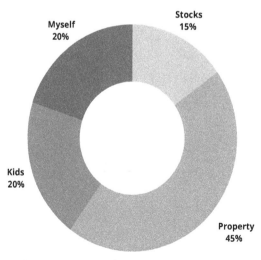

Myself 20%
Stocks 15%
Kids 20%
Property 45%

MODULE FOUR

CAREER
FIND BALANCE & SUCCESS IN YOUR WORK

MODULES

1. ALIGN YOUR VALUES
2. ALIGN YOUR SKILLS & GENERATE INCOME
3. LIFESTYLE DESIGN

KNOWING YOUR VALUES

IMPORTANCE OF VALUES

If the choices and decisions you are making day to day are in line with your core values then you can stop worrying about the future, you don't need instant results when you are content in knowing you are on the way to becoming the person you want to become

VALUES ALIGNMENT

COMMON KEY VALUES	YOUR KEY VALUES	ALIGNED
STABILITY	STABILITY	✓
CONTRIBUTION		☐
CHALLENGE		☐
VARIETY		☐
SUCCESS		☐
FUN		☐
RELATIONSHIPS		☐
FAMILY		☐
INTEGRITY		☐

ARE THE MAJORITY OF YOUR VALUES ALIGNED WITH YOUR CURRENT WORK?   YES ☐   NO ☐

CHOOSING A LINE OF WORK

PART 1. SKILLS ALIGNMENT

COMMON KEY SKILLS	YOUR KEY SKILLS	ALIGNED
MULTITASKING	MULTITASKING	☑
PEOPLE		☐
LEADING		☐
MANAGING		☐
DETAIL ORIENTED		☐
ANALYTICAL		☐
AUTONOMOUS		☐
DECISION MAKING		☐
SALES		☐

ARE THE MAJORITY OF YOUR SKILLS ALIGNED WITH YOUR CURRENT WORK?   YES ☐   NO ☐

PART 2. THE NUMBER

AT SOME POINT IN THE FUTURE, WILL MY CURRENT LINE OF WORK OR BUSINESS PROVIDE ME WITH THE OPPORTUNITY TO EARN THE INCOME THAT I DESIRE WHILST LIVING THE LIFESTYLE THAT I WANT?   YES ☐   NO ☐

LIFESTYLE DESIGN

FACTOR	WORK LIFE CHECKLIST	YES
1	YOU ARE SOMEWHAT PASSIONATE ABOUT YOUR WORK	☐
2	YOU ENJOY THE PEOPLE YOU WORK WITH	☐
3	YOU HAVE FLEXIBLE WORKING ARRANGEMENTS	☐
4	YOUR JOB INVOLVES HELPING PEOPLE IN SOME CAPACITY	☐
5	YOUR WORK ISN'T GRINDING YOU INTO THE GROUND	☐
6	YOU CAN SEE GROWTH IN YOUR CAREER	☐
7	YOU HAVE THE ABILITY TO BE THE BEST IN YOUR FIELD	☐
8	YOU HAVE THE ABILITY TO TAKE TIME OFF AND ENJOY THE RIDE	☐
9	YOUR CAREER IS GOING TO GIVE YOU THE INCOME YOU NEED FOR YOUR IDEAL LIFE	☐

TO ENSURE YOU ARE ABLE TO FIND BALANCE IN YOUR WORK AND ARE MAXIMISING YOUR POTENTIAL YOU SHOULD BE ABLE TO TICK AT LEAST 5-6 OUT OF 9 BOXES HERE

CAREER ACCELERATOR PLAN

ACTION PLAN

YES

1 I KNOW THE NEW SKILLS I NEED TO DEVELOP TO TO TAKE MY BUSINESS OR CAREER TO THE NEXT LEVEL ☐

2 I HAVE FOUND A MENTOR AND SOMEONE WHO I ASPIRE TO REPLICATE ☐

3 I AM COMMITTED TO TO THE THREE YEAR PUSH ☐

4 I WILL REFUSE TO SETTLE ☐

5 I'LL PLAY THE LONG GAME AND FOCUS LONG TERM NOT SHORT TERM ☐

6 I KNOW THE PEOPLE I NEED TO CONNECT WITH TO TAKE MY BUSINESS OR CAREER TO THE NEXT LEVEL ☐

7 I WILL AIM TO DO GOOD AS I TRY AND DO WELL ☐

8 I'LL DO MORE THAN IM PAID FOR ☐

9 I'LL MAKE IT TO THE TOP THE RIGHT WAY, I'LL BRING OTHERS WITH ME ☐

THANK YOU

IF YOU WOULD LIKE 1 ON 1 TRAINING HEAD OVER TO TONYCAINE.COM

NOTES